First Edition published by Impact Investment Partners 2024

First Edition

THE LONG GAME

The 20-Year Roadmap to Building Tax-Free Wealth Through Scalable Real Estate Strategies

Burke Atkerson

Table of contents

Preface

Six years ago, we found ourselves broke and at a crossroads. Coming from almost a decade in South America where beans and rice were staples in our missionary budget, we returned to the States, not just to reclaim the life we left behind, but to save our marriage. I remember arriving at the DFW with my wife and children, 4 suit cases and a $4,000 to our name. We had nearly nothing. It was a humbling moment, returning to the life we had paused, only to find our peers miles ahead, their lives seemingly well-constructed with tangible assets and homes that spoke of their success.

We felt behind, almost as if we had been left out of a race we never knew we were running. But this wasn't just about catching up; it was about setting a new path for ourselves. With our marriage being rebuilt on a new foundation, we ventured into the unknown territory of real estate. It began with real estate sales, a step into the waters of a complex industry. Then, as we found our footing, we began to do fix and flips, learning the ropes one property at a time.

The real game-changer was apartment syndication. It wasn't just about buying property; it was about creating opportunities, not just for us but for others through our firm Impact Investment Partners. We are driven by the various positive impacts we get to make. We began to raise capital, bringing accredited investors together, and began to scale our portfolio in ways we hadn't imagined possible.

Yet, despite these strides, I often find myself battling the imposter syndrome, questioning our rightful place in this journey. I’ve experienced lots of success but I am still quite short of where I will be 20 years from now. And that long-term perspective is exactly the point of this book.

This path has been anything but easy. The real estate market is a relentless teacher, with market cycles that can humble you overnight. But it's in this relentless pursuit of mastery, of understanding the ebbs and flows, that we've found our place. We're not just building a portfolio; we're building a legacy of generosity, one that's measured not in the immediate returns but in the wealth that compounds over decades and brims over into the world around us.

This book I write not just from my experience and successes but from my failures as well. This is a guide for you, crafted from the lessons learned in the trenches of real estate, designed for those who are willing to embrace the slow burn of success. It's for you, the reader, who sees beyond the immediate gratification of today and is willing to invest in the vision of what lies twenty, thirty years ahead.

Real estate is a compounding business. The initial years are tough, marked by delayed gratification and the kind of slow, painstaking growth that can test your resolve. But if you stay the course with grit, if you learn from the market and your mistakes, you'll find yourself on the path to massive equity and wealth that truly lasts.

This journey isn't for the faint of heart. It's for those willing to grow, to endure, and to invest in a future that's built on solid ground. As you turn these pages, know that the path ahead is one of profound opportunity, paved by the lessons of those who've walked it before you. Welcome to the journey of real estate investment, where the true reward lies not just in the destination, but in the growth and resilience fostered along the way.

RICH VS WEALTHY

My own journey in real estate investment began with a revelation that shifted my view of wealth. In my first sales meeting at a Berkshire Hathaway HomeServices branch, the supervising broker, earning over $1 million annually, shared a perspective that broadened my financial understanding. Despite his high income as a successful business owner and broker in Colorado, he stated, "*I am rich, but I am not wealthy. Do you know the difference? Rich people still have to work for their income.*"

This statement struck me deeply. Here was someone with considerable financial success, yet he differentiated between being rich and being wealthy. This distinction highlighted that true wealth isn't just about earnings, but how those earnings are made and used. It's about developing a system where your wealth generates more wealth, independently of your direct labor.

You are wealthy when your assets work for you, allowing you to focus on what truly matters. Wealth isn't just about the amount of money you have; it's about the freedom it grants you. It's the ability to live life according to your own rules, making choices driven by joy, fulfillment, and the desire to build a lasting legacy. Wealth enables you to make a significant impact in the world. This book is for people like you and me, eager to grow and change what's not working. It invites you on a journey from simply being rich to becoming truly wealthy, where your money works for you, creating a legacy for future generations.

The distinction between being rich and truly wealthy is significant and often misunderstood. Being rich might mean having a high income, a luxurious lifestyle, and impressive assets. Yet, as "The Millionaire Next Door" shows, even high-earning professionals can struggle to accumulate real wealth. Surprisingly, only about 2% reach millionaire status. The main issue? Overspending because of high income, leading to a cycle where even large earnings are outpaced by increasing expenses. This pattern not only blocks wealth accumulation but also prevents passing it on to future generations, as high spending becomes a family norm.

Today, being a millionaire does not mean you're wealthy. If the highest W2 earners struggle to build wealth, who succeeds? The answer lies in those who have understood the essence of true wealth creation. They are the ones who have left the rat race and embraced the mindset of billionaires.

Throughout this book, we will explore how innovators and leaders have not only accumulated wealth but used it to create significant and lasting impacts. These individuals have redefined the concept of wealth, moving from the traditional narrative of working for money to a paradigm where money serves their vision and legacy.

Welcome to your journey from Rich to Wealthy. It's a path that will challenge your perceptions, transform your financial strategies, and lead you to a place where wealth isn't just an abundance of resources, but an abundance of choices, freedom, and legacy.

WHY REAL ESTATE

In a moment that illuminated the corridors of financial wisdom and strategy, two titans of entrepreneurship and investment, Robert Herjavec and Grant Cardone, found themselves in a discussion that would reveal a profound truth about wealth creation through real estate.

Robert Herjavec, known for his razor-sharp business acumen and an impressive net worth of $300 million, was posed a question that would make many ponder the foundations of their financial strategies. The question was simple yet profound: "If you were down to your last million dollars, would you be able to get wealthy again? How would you do it?"

Without a moment's hesitation, Herjavec's response was as clear as it was insightful. "If I were down to my last million, I would invest it in something real estate," he declared. This statement wasn't just a reflection of a personal preference but a strategic choice that has stood the test of time in the world of investment.

The interviewer, none other than Grant Cardone, himself a behemoth in the realm of real estate with a staggering net worth of about $4.6 billion, couldn't help but agree wholeheartedly. "I 100% agree. Why Real Estate?" he inquired, nudging the conversation deeper into the philosophy of investment.

Herjavec's reply was a masterclass in investment strategy. "You have to take desperation out of the equation," he began, highlighting the importance of removing financial pressure to make sound investment decisions. He elaborated on the unique advantage of real estate investments, noting, "You can purchase real estate that provides passive income, and then you have income to pay your bills while you build wealth."

This strategy, according to Herjavec, not only offers a buffer against immediate financial pressures but also lays the groundwork for long-term wealth accumulation. As real estate properties appreciate in value, they build equity, enhancing the investor's wealth portfolio over time.

Herjavec's approach encapsulates a key principle in wealth creation: investing in assets that not only provide immediate returns but also appreciate in value, ensuring a dual pathway to financial growth. This methodical approach to investment underscores the power of real estate as a vehicle for wealth creation, capable of transforming financial landscapes and securing futures.

Real estate is the proven path to life-changing wealth. It’s a field that has consistently demonstrated its capacity to transform ordinary financial landscapes into extraordinary legacies. Unlike other investment options, real estate offers a unique blend of stability, tangible assets, and long-term growth potential. It stands as the cornerstone in wealth-building, providing a reliable and often lucrative path to not only accumulate significant wealth but also maintain and increase it over time.

Nearly every billionaire in the US incorporates real estate as a crucial component in their investment portfolio, recognizing it as a key tool for both building and preserving their wealth. Real estate offers a unique combination of stable value appreciation, potential for passive income, and diversification, which is essential for managing risk. This asset class, with its tangible nature and often predictable market trends, provides a solid foundation for long-term wealth accumulation and security. For these ultra-wealthy individuals, real estate is not just an investment; it's a strategic choice for sustained financial growth and wealth preservation.

MAKING THE MOST OF TAX BENEFITS

These real estate stars also shine in how they handle taxes. They use tax benefits smartly, showing deep knowledge of how to protect and grow their wealth. This part of their story is not just about managing money—it’s about opening up a world of possibilities. It encourages us, as investors, to really understand wealth preservation and growth.

In the next chapters, we'll reveal the tax strategies they used. We’ll learn how you can use the Tax Code to not only build but also protect your wealth for generations. This is more than finance tips; it's a way to make your dreams come true and build a lasting legacy.

In this book, we focus mainly on real estate, despite the important role businesses play in building wealth. We chose real estate because of its unique features as an investment. It’s not just about making money; it’s a strong base for long-term wealth. The tax perks of real estate can really speed up wealth building. These benefits not only complement business operations; they enhance them. The tax breaks you get with real estate can reduce or even wipe out the taxes usually linked with running a business, making your strategy to accumulate wealth more effective.

THIS IS YOUR PLAYBOOK

In the pages of this book, you're about to embark on a journey that changes not just your life but generations after you as well. It's not merely about accumulating riches; it's about architecting a legacy that transcends the here and now, extending far into the future. This book is your roadmap, your strategic guide to navigating the complex terrain of wealth creation through the power of real estate investment.

Wealth cannot materialize overnight. It's the culmination of years, often decades, of strategic planning, smart decisions, delayed gratification, and unwavering commitment to a vision that stretches 15-25 years into the future. Take a moment to envision what you want your life to look like two decades from now. This book is designed to help you reverse engineer that vision, transforming it from a distant dream into a tangible reality.

Begin with the end in mind. **Part 1: Laying the Foundation** is where the journey begins. This initial phase is about more than just understanding the mechanics of real estate investment; it's about cultivating the right mindset for wealth building. It's here that we set the cornerstones of gratitude, growth, and strategic thinking. This foundation is crucial; it's the bedrock upon which all future success will be built. Whether you're starting with ample capital or just a reservoir of ambition, this phase is where you prepare yourself for the journey ahead.

As we transition into **Part 2: Multiplication and Diversification**, the scope of our journey expands. Here, the seeds sown in the foundational phase begin to sprout, opening up avenues for growth and expansion. This phase is characterized by the strategic multiplication of your assets and the diversification of your investment portfolio. From niche real estate sectors to multifamily investments, this phase is about broadening your horizons and solidifying your footprint in the real estate market.

Next is **Part 3: Efficiency At-Scale**. It's where your investments begin to yield their full potential, optimized for tax efficiency and scaled to a level where your wealth begins to generate more wealth at an explosive level. **This is the phase that reveals the secret strategies billionaires use to expand and preserve their wealth. This phase is the epitome of wealth. It's where you get your time back because your money does the work for you.** This is the pinnacle of real estate investment, where strategic planning and smart decision-making come to fruition, allowing you to achieve not just wealth but generational wealth.

We conclude our journey together in **Part 4: Long-Term Planning.** This section unpacks the more-than 6000 page tax code to help you utilize the same strategies that Billionaires use to build and preserve wealth. And in the final chapter I show you how to put everything we've discussed into a personalized actionable plan for building life-changing wealth.

This book is not just about navigating the complexities of real estate investment; it's about charting a course for your future, a future where your wealth serves not just your immediate needs but the needs of generations to come. So, as we embark on this journey together, remember: the path to generational wealth is a marathon, not a sprint. It requires patience, perseverance, and a vision that extends decades and generations out.

PART 1: LAYING THE FOUNDATION

ONE

THE BILLIONAIRE MINDSET

***

Wealth doesn't begin with your bank account; it begins in your mind. The journey to financial success is shaped by the thoughts, beliefs, and attitudes that influence our view of money. In this chapter I invite you on a journey of transformation, shifting your thinking from just making money to mindfully creating wealth.

Consider Andrew Carnegie's advice: "The person who learns to fully control their mind can control anything else they rightfully deserve." This idea guides us in mastering our mindset. By developing a way of thinking that sees opportunities in challenges and finds solutions in problems, we build a strong base not only for financial wealth but for a life filled with satisfaction and impact.

Think about this: What ideas about wealth were part of your early life? How do these influence your financial decisions now? Understanding and changing your financial mindset is the first step to changing your story about wealth.

This section helps you navigate the world of wealth, guiding you towards a mindset that values plenty, grabs opportunities, and stays resilient. It's about moving from a scarcity mindset, where money is a worry, to a mindset of abundance, where wealth is a tool for positive change and personal satisfaction.

THE ALCHEMY OF GIVING

True wealth is measured not by what you accumulate, but by what you give away. The idea of giving more than you receive isn't just about being kind; it's a smart strategy for lasting success. By providing great value to others, you set a strong foundation for long-term achievement and happiness.

Having a mindset focused on service changes what success means. It's not just about what you earn, but what you give. In real estate, business, or everyday life, aim to give more in value than what you receive in payment. This way, you create strong relationships, build goodwill, and often set the stage for bigger, lasting success. It's about starting a cycle where your success helps others, which in turn boosts your own success.

CONSTANT GROWTH

Your financial growth reflects your personal development. Carol Dweck's concept of a Growth Mindset might seem overused in the business world, and you might be tired of hearing about it. However, it's essential for wealth building, a skill few truly master. This mindset embraces the idea that your abilities and intelligence can evolve over time. It encourages you to confront challenges directly, persist through setbacks, and view hard work as a route to mastery. Imagine facing a significant failure in a real estate investment that seemed promising. The easy reaction might be to think real estate investing isn't your forte, or that you should stick to what you're already good at. This kind of thinking is more common than you might think. With a growth mindset, however, you'd approach the same failure with a renewed determination to understand what went wrong, learn from it, and keep moving forward.

As you step into this new path of wealth creation, a growth mindset is your most valuable tool. Your failures are your most valuable assets. Learn to learn from your mistakes, adapt to changes, and continually refine your investment strategies. This approach involves recognizing growth opportunities in every situation and having the tenacity to chase them. Remember, investing is inherently unpredictable, and mistakes are an inevitable part of the journey. The real question is, how will you respond when you face them?

VISUALIZATION: CRAFTING YOUR BILLIONAIRE MINDSET

Imagine your best self and start being that person. Industry giant Andrew Carnegie credited much of his success to what he called creative vision. Visualization is about clearly picturing the peak of your goals and dreams. It's a crucial method for aligning your deepest desires with your active goals, and vice versa.

Creative visualization goes beyond simple daydreaming. It involves actively imagining yourself at your most successful. If you can't see yourself reaching billionaire status, it's much harder to achieve it. This practice is key in setting ambitious goals and mentally preparing to handle success. Without this mental framework, even temporary high success can be lost due to inner conflict, as your mind struggles to adapt to this new reality of wealth and success.

Thomas Edison's invention of the light bulb is a classic example of resilience and visualization. Inventing the light bulb wasn't easy; it was a tough journey filled with many failures. Each failure taught Edison something new, bringing him closer to his goal.

Edison's persistence was driven by a clear and strong vision. Despite many setbacks, he never lost sight of his main goal: a working, efficient electric light bulb. His experience shows the power of a growth mindset and visualization. Despite failures, Edison's belief in his vision was unshakeable. His famous quote, "I have not failed. I've just found 10,000 ways that won't work," shows his dedication and belief in learning.

The breakthrough in Edison's work came when he noticed how air flow affected heat and light. This insight, from his sharp observation and innovative thinking, led to the vital invention of a vacuum-sealed bulb with a carbon filament. This moment turned his vision into reality, showing the incredible power of combining a clear vision with persistent effort.

GET-RICH-QUICK QUICKLY FAILS

Embrace patience and foresight, for they are the silent guardians of lasting wealth. In the building of wealth, delayed gratification is the keystone holding it all together. Choosing long-term gains over immediate rewards isn't merely a strategy; it's an essential mindset for sustainable financial growth. It involves understanding the compounding power of patience and the strategic value of investment.

In every wealth-building journey, decisions involve a trade-off between immediate benefits and long-term potential. Consider the real estate market: the quick profits from flipping a house may seem attractive, but they often overshadow the long-term benefits and stable income that come from owning rental properties. While immediate profits are appealing, they also bring challenges like higher taxes and missing out on long-term appreciation and steady cash flow.

The real worth of assets like rental properties becomes clear over time. As rental incomes rise and mortgages decrease, these investments turn into major sources of income and equity. This shift from immediate cash to long-term wealth is what strategic wealth building is all about. It means making choices now that lay the groundwork for significant growth and financial security later on.

Building lasting wealth is like growing a tree; it requires patience and care to eventually enjoy its benefits. It's about planning for the future, knowing that the real value of an investment often shows itself with time. This long-term view is essential for anyone serious about not just making but keeping and increasing their wealth.

The idea of getting rich quickly is often misleading and can lead to financial mistakes. Real, lasting wealth is built through hard work, a clear vision, smart decisions, and a strong commitment. It's a path marked by steady effort and the ability to adapt to changing financial situations.

Wisdom is vital in this journey. It comes from a mix of knowledge, experience, and a deep understanding of risks and rewards. It's about making decisions based on what you've learned from past successes and failures and continually seeking more knowledge. The road to financial success is rarely straightforward or easy; it requires the resolve to stay on track and the strength to face challenges.

Being able to adapt is critical in the ever-changing world of finance and investment. The ability to shift strategies in response to market changes, economic trends, and personal life events is key to maintaining and growing your wealth. It's about staying flexible and responsive to economic shifts, ensuring your wealth-building strategies are strong and adaptable.

YOU ARE ALREADY RICH

Gratitude is the foundation of wealth. As we chase financial success, we often overlook life's real treasures – those priceless things that money can't buy. Think about it: would you take $10 million tonight if it meant not waking up tomorrow? Most likely, your answer is no. This shows that the value of each day you live is immeasurable, far beyond millions.

This understanding opens up a new perspective on wealth. Your life is already rich, regardless of how much money you have. If you're alive and breathing today, you have something priceless. The presence of friends, family, or even just one positive thing in your life is a richness that money can't match.

Reflect on this: Every sunrise is a day worth more than $10 million to you. This isn't just a poetic idea; it's a powerful reality check about the value of life and the many kinds of wealth we have. I encourage you to appreciate the richness of your life – the relationships, experiences, and simple joys that create a truly wealthy existence.

On this journey, take time to recognize the non-monetary riches in your life. What blessings, big or small, make your daily life better? What brings you joy, fulfillment, and purpose? Exploring these isn't just being thankful; it's a shift in how you see the world. It's about seeing and valuing the various forms of wealth you already have.

Recognizing and valuing these parts of your life builds a foundation of happiness and abundance. It changes your focus from what you don't have to what you do, creating a mindset that's ready to attract and grow more wealth. This isn't about putting aside your financial goals; it's about enhancing your path to those goals with a deeper appreciation for the wealth you already have in your life.

Take a moment to really think about this. It's actually the most important idea in this entire book.

BEYOND MONEY

Imagine a life where wealth is no longer a pursuit, but a companion. Think about it: what does a truly rich life mean to you - independent of financial constraints? If money were no object, how would you sculpt your days? What activities would fill your hours? How would it feel to live in that reality? Write down what you discover.

This exploration isn't a mere daydream; it's a practice in understanding your deepest values and aspirations. It's about painting a vivid picture of your ideal life – one that resonates with your innermost desires and passions.

Visualize your perfect day. From the moment you wake up to the time you lay your head to rest, what does this day encompass? Are you surrounded by nature or immersed in creative pursuits? Are you spending invaluable time with loved ones, exploring new hobbies, or perhaps contributing to a cause close to your heart?

Beyond the activities, delve into the feelings and emotions that this ideal life evokes. Is it a sense of peace, joy, fulfillment, or perhaps a combination of these? How does it feel to live a life aligned with your true desires, free from financial constraints?

This mental exercise is not an escape from reality; it's a compass pointing towards your true north. What themes emerge from your envisioned day? Do they highlight a love for adventure, a passion for art, or a dedication to community and relationships? These themes are the essence of your rich life, guiding your decisions and shaping your path to wealth.

With this clear vision, you can begin to align your wealth-building strategies to support this ideal life. It's about creating wealth not as an end in itself but as a means to live your richest life. This vision serves as a beacon, guiding your financial decisions and investments towards creating a life that is not just financially abundant but abundantly fulfilling.

This is how you craft a life where wealth serves your deepest aspirations, not where your aspirations are confined by wealth. This is also the first step to aligning your actions with your financial goals. If you can’t visualize it, you can’t achieve it.

TWO

BEGINNING TO BUILD CAPITAL

Four years ago, my financial situation was far from impressive. With only two thousand dollars in our bank account and a credit line that was anything but extensive, my spouse and I stood on the brink of a decision that would change our lives forever. We were faced with an opportunity in real estate, a fix and flip that felt more like a distant dream than an achievable goal.

The first hurdle was capital. Traditional avenues were closed to us, given our financial situation. So, I reached out to a friend, hopeful for a loan to cover the down payment. His hesitant response, "Let me talk to my wife about it," was a gentle reminder of the risks involved, not just financially but personally. Two days later, he kindly declined, citing the potential risk to our friendship. I assume he was also concerned with my lack of experience. I would have been too.

Undeterred, I found another way. An unsecured personal loan, typically used for buying cars or consolidating debt, became the unlikely lifeline for our venture. With forty thousand dollars secured, we purchased our first fix and flip. The process was full of challenges, learning curves, and moments of doubt. I am no handyman and learning about construction was even harder than figuring out financing. Three months later, we emerged not just successful but transformed. The project netted us a profit of over thirty thousand dollars, proving that with the right mindset, determination, and a willingness to take calculated risks, even the most ambitious dreams are within reach.

That first flip was the beginning of what would become a journey of growth, learning, and ultimately, building a turnkey fix-and-flip company and a construction company for investors. Today my team has over a hundred flips under out belt, the path from zero capital to a thriving real estate money-printing machine is not just a testament to our persistence but a blueprint for anyone looking to do the same.

This chapter is not about my journey; it's about showing you that building capital in real estate, even when you start with none, is not only possible but achievable. This chapter is dedicated to debunking the myth that entering real estate requires substantial capital. Here, we explore strategies that enable you to start building wealth in real estate, regardless of your current financial standing. If you're already well-capitalized and ready to leap into larger investments, feel free to advance to the next chapter. But if you're starting with little to no capital, this chapter is your blueprint for getting started with explosive traction.

LEVERAGE IN REAL ESTATE

Before diving into specific strategies, it's crucial to understand the concept of leverage in real estate. Leverage, in simple terms, is the use of borrowed capital for investment, with the expectation that the profits made will be greater than the interest payable. In real estate, this can mean using a mortgage to purchase a property. The key here is that you control a valuable asset without fully paying for it upfront. This is the cornerstone of real estate investment and a tool that can be wielded effectively, even by those starting with minimal funds.

STRATEGY 1: WHOLESALING

Wholesaling is a prime strategy for entering the real estate market without significant capital. It involves entering into a contract with a seller and then assigning that contract to an end buyer for a fee. That fee is often times $5,000 to $50,000. Do one deal per month and you can make decent income. However, notice that this is active work, and it is not investing. Here's how to do it effectively:

1. **Understand Your Market**: Know the neighborhoods, types of properties, and price points that are in demand. Use tools like the MLS (Multiple Listing Service), local real estate websites, and public records.

2. **Build a Network**: Connect with local real estate investors, agents, and potential buyers. Attend real estate meetups and investor groups to build these connections.

3. **Marketing for Deals**: Use bandit signs, direct mail campaigni s, online ads, or even drive around neighborhoods to look for distressed properties.

4. **Estimate Repair Costs**: Learn to accurately estimate repair costs, which will be crucial for negotiating deals and presenting them to buyers.

5. **Draft an Effective Assignment Contract**: Work with a real estate attorney to create a solid assignment contract that protects your interests.

We don't recommend spending too much time and energy doing wholesaling Although there is little to no risk in wholsaling, it is time intensive. Instead focus your energy on the last strategy discussed here: Fix & flips.

STRATEGY 2: MICRO-INVESTING IN REAL ESTATE

Micro-investing in real estate, facilitated by a range of online platforms, presents an accessible entry point for many aspiring investors. These platforms democratize real estate investment, breaking down traditional barriers to entry by allowing investments in small, manageable amounts. However, while micro-investing offers an easy start, it's crucial to understand its limitations, particularly in terms of leverage and potential returns.

While micro-investing in real estate has gained popularity as an accessible means for individuals to dip their toes into the property market, it's important to critically assess this approach. After careful consideration, I recommend avoiding micro-investing in real estate altogether, primarily due to its lack of leverage and the potential risks that mirror those found in trading and gambling.

THE CORE ISSUES WITH MICRO-INVESTING

1. **Absence of Leverage**: One of the greatest powers in real estate investment is the ability to use leverage — that is, using borrowed capital to increase the potential return of an investment. Micro-investing, by its nature, doesn't employ leverage. Investors use their own money to buy small shares in properties, significantly limiting the potential for substantial returns.

2. **Reduced Control and Influence**: Micro-investors typically have little to no say in the management or strategic decisions regarding the properties they invest in. This lack of control can be a significant downside, as real estate investment often benefits from hands-on management and strategic decision-making.

3. **Risk of Speculative Mindset**: The ease and accessibility of micro-investing platforms can encourage a more casual, less disciplined approach to investment. This mindset can lead to decisions that are more speculative in nature, akin to gambling or stock market trading, rather than grounded in solid real estate fundamentals.

4. **Diluted Returns**: Given that investments are typically spread across various properties and investors, the returns on individual investments can be quite diluted. While this spreads risk, it also means that successful investments yield lower returns to individual investors.

A BETTER PATH TO REAL ESTATE INVESTMENT

For those serious about building wealth through real estate, more traditional investment methods are advisable. These methods offer greater potential for return, more control, and the invaluable advantage of leveraging. Strategies such as direct property ownership, whether in residential or commercial real estate, provide the opportunity to make strategic decisions that can significantly impact the investment's success.

For those aiming to build serious wealth through real estate, focusing on traditional investment methods and avoiding the allure of micro-investing is a more prudent approach. By embracing strategies that allow for leverage, control, and strategic influence, investors can unlock the true potential of real estate and pave the way for significant financial growth and stability.

STRATEGY 3: LAND FLIPPING

Land flipping is a distinctive strategy in the real estate investment landscape, involving the purchase and subsequent resale of undeveloped land for profit. This method can be particularly appealing for its relatively low-risk profile and the flexibility it offers, allowing investors to operate remotely.

Land flipping centers on identifying, purchasing, and reselling land. The process involves several key steps:

1.

In-Depth Market Research: This is the cornerstone of successful land flipping. Understanding the potential for growth and development in various regions is crucial. This research can often be conducted remotely, using online resources to analyze market trends, future development plans, and land values.

2. **Acquisition**: The next phase involves acquiring the land. This could be through direct purchases, auctions, or tax lien sales. The goal is to find land that is undervalued or has potential for appreciation.

3. **Value Enhancement**: While the land is typically sold as it is, its value can be increased through obtaining permits, rezoning, or simply clearing and preparing the land for development.

4. **Selling**: The final step is selling the land for a profit. This could involve working with real estate agents or directly reaching out to potential buyers like developers or investors.

THE BENEFITS OF LAND FLIPPING

- **Low Risk**: One of the primary advantages of land flipping is its relatively low-risk nature. Unlike properties with structures, land does not usually depreciate due to structural issues or wear and tear. Additionally, the land market tends to be less volatile than the housing market, making it a more stable investment option.

-

Remote Operation: Land flipping can often be done remotely. With the right research tools and resources, you can identify and analyze potential land purchases from anywhere in the country. This flexibility allows investors to tap into different markets without the need to be physically present.

- **Simple Due diligence:** Dealing with undeveloped land generally involves fewer complications than developed properties. There are no buildings to inspect, no tenants to manage, and no renovations to undertake.

While land flipping presents unique opportunities in the real estate market with its low-risk nature and potential for remote operation, it's important to exercise caution, especially for first-time investors. This strategy, though lucrative in certain situations, carries specific challenges and nuances that might not make it the ideal starting point for newcomers to real estate investing.

CONSIDERATIONS FOR FIRST-TIME INVESTORS

- **Complex Financing**: Acquiring financing for land purchases can be more complicated than financing developed properties. Lenders often view land as a riskier investment, leading to stricter lending criteria and potentially higher interest rates. This complexity in securing funds can be a significant barrier for first-time investors.

- **Illiquidity**: One of the critical risks associated with land flipping is the potential lack of liquidity. Unlike residential or commercial properties, which generally have a more active and consistent market, selling undeveloped land can take much longer. This extended timeframe can tie up funds and limit the ability to pursue other investment opportunities.

- **Absence of Forced Equity**: Unlike property flipping or rentals where value can be added through improvements or development, land flipping typically lacks the ability to force equity. The profit in land flipping often hinges on market trends or changes in land use regulations, factors that are largely outside an investor's control.

- **Arbitrage vs. Investment**: Land flipping can be more accurately described as a form of arbitrage rather than true investment. It involves capitalizing on price differences in the market rather than adding value or generating income through development or rental. This approach requires a keen understanding of market dynamics and trends, which might be challenging for those new to real estate.

A WORD OF CAUTION

For those just beginning their journey in real estate investing, starting with more straightforward strategies such as residential property investments might be more advantageous. These avenues offer clearer paths to financing, more straightforward ways to add value (and hence force equity), and generally provide more liquidity. They also allow new investors to gain experience in the real estate market with a relatively lower risk profile.

Land flipping, while an intriguing option within the real estate spectrum, may not be the best fit for first-time investors due to its complexity in financing, potential liquidity issues, and reliance on market arbitrage. It’s a strategy better suited for those who already have some experience in real estate and can navigate its unique challenges. For beginners, focusing on more traditional and straightforward real estate investments is advisable, saving land flipping for a later stage when they have more experience and resources to effectively manage its intricacies.

STRATEGY 3: FIX & FLIP

Doing fix and flips is the single most powerful way to build capital using real estate - especially for those starting with limited or no initial funds. This strategy revolves around buying properties at a lower price, renovating them, and then selling them for a profit. It's a method that requires insight, planning, and a bit of creativity, but the potential returns make it a compelling option.

THE LEVERAGING ADVANTAGE

One of the most compelling aspects of fix and flips is the ability to use leverage effectively. By utilizing borrowed capital, primarily through hard money loans, investors can finance a substantial part of the purchase and renovation costs. This method significantly reduces the personal capital required to initiate a project, making it accessible for individuals who may not have extensive savings but possess a solid credit history. The beauty of leverage in real estate lies in its capacity to magnify returns on investment. It allows investors to control a valuable asset and potentially sell it at a significant profit, relative to their initial personal investment.

INJECTING EQUITY AND ADDING VALUE

Beyond the financial mechanics, fix and flips involve a transformative process – turning undervalued and often neglected properties into desirable homes. This transformation isn't merely cosmetic; it often includes substantial improvements that enhance both the functionality and appeal of the property. The renovation process effectively injects equity into these properties. The difference between the combined costs of purchase and renovation and the new, higher selling price is where the profit lies. This added value is the primary driver of return in fix and flip investments.

MEETING HOMEBUYER NEEDS AND REVITALIZING COMMUNITIES

The value of fix and flips extends into the social realm, addressing real needs in the housing market. Many homebuyers, echoing your own experience, seek homes that are updated and ready for immediate occupation. They often lack the time, expertise, or financial resources to undertake significant renovations. Flippers fulfill this market demand by offering modern, functional living spaces without the premium price tag of new constructions.

Furthermore, fix and flips contribute to the revitalization of neighborhoods. Each renovated property can elevate the aesthetic and functional quality of the area, enhancing the overall value and appeal of the community. This not only benefits current residents but also attracts new interest to the neighborhood, fostering a positive cycle of investment and improvement.

THE ECONOMIC AND SOCIAL RIPPLE EFFECT

Fix and flip projects stimulate local economies by creating jobs and demand for materials and services. They also encourage more investments in the area, leading to broader economic and social upliftment. Moreover, the profits from flipping are not just a reward for buying and selling property; they also compensate for the expertise, effort, and risk management involved in transforming a property. Flippers invest time and resources in understanding market trends, managing renovation projects, and often engaging in hands-on work to bring a vision to fruition.

BALANCING RISK AND REWARD

It's important to acknowledge that with the potential for high returns comes a degree of risk. Flippers take on the market's volatility, unexpected renovation challenges, and the intricacies of managing a complex project. However, it's this very balance of risk and reward that makes fix and flips a dynamic and potentially lucrative venture in the real estate domain.

FINDING A DEAL

1. **Market Research**: Understanding your local real estate market is key. Identify areas with high potential for growth or neighborhoods in the process of gentrification.

2. **Networking**: Build relationships with real estate agents, other flippers, wholesalers, and anyone familiar with the real estate market. Real estate meetups and online forums can be great places to start.

3. **Property Hunting**: Look for properties that are undervalued and in need of repairs that you can manage. Foreclosures, auction properties, and distressed sales are often good candidates.

FINANCING THE DEAL

1. **Earnest Money**: This initial deposit can often be borrowed. The key is to have a good deal in hand which makes lenders more willing to provide these funds.

2. **Hard Money Lenders**: These lenders typically finance 90% the purchase price and 100% the rehab costs. They usually focus on the property's potential and the deal's merit rather than your personal financial situation.

3. **Additional Funding Sources**: If there's a shortfall, it can be covered through savings, private money lenders, credit cards, or a business line of credit. The flexibility in funding is one of the major advantages of fix and flips.

ANALYZING THE DEAL

1. **After Repair Value (ARV)**: Determine the property's potential value after renovations. This involves researching similar properties in the area and their sale prices. You can ask a Realtor contact in that market to run comps for you for similar fully-renovated properties.

2. **Simple Profitability Calculation**: Take the ARV, subtract the acquisition cost, subtract the estimated rehab budget, and subtract transaction costs. Multiply that number by 0.35. That is your estimated profit on the deal. What to look for is $30,000 or more in profit. If the market is volatile or dropping, you want that minimum profit number to be closer to $50,000. If the market is increasing, you can lower that

number to $20,000. But $30,000 is a good number in most situations.

3. **The 70% Rule:** A rule of thumb that used to be used by real estate flippers, is the 70% rule. Take 70% of the ARV and subtract the rehab budget. That is your highest offer price. Lenders like this rule because it is safe. But be warned: this rule does not work most of the time. In tiny towns where you can find ridiculous deals, it might be a little more common. But in emerging markets and cities that are appreciating in value, it is much more difficult to come across a deal like this. Use the $30,000 rule instead.

4. **Reality TV:** Realty shows about flipping houses are anything but reality. Fiction is a much more fitting description. Do not expect to make $70,000+ on your flips like you see on TV. Those deals come around every once in a while, but don't expect to hit home runs on every deal. Aim to make $30,000 or more. This number allows you enough margin to dip into in the case of unexpected expenses. And it is small enough to do a high volume of flips in your market every year.

PRACTICAL STEPS FOR SUCCESSFUL FIX & FLIPS

Step 1: Deal Analysis

- **Educate Yourself**: Learn how to accurately calculate ARV and understand the costs involved in purchasing and rehabbing a property.

-

Use Technology: Utilize real estate analysis tools and software to help estimate costs and potential returns.

Step 2: Financing

- **Hard Money Loans**: Research and connect with reputable hard money lenders. Understand their terms and conditions.

- **Negotiate Terms**: Work to secure the best terms for your loan, including interest rates and repayment schedules.

Step 3: Renovation

- **Budgeting**: Create a detailed budget for the renovation. Factor in all costs, including unexpected expenses.

- **Contractor Relations**: Build relationships with cheap contractors and subcontractors. Get multiple quotes and check references before hiring. Most people don't realize that there are two kinds of residential contractors, even though they would never market themselves as such: retail contractors and wholesale contractors. Retail contractors have well established businesses and clientelle. They do not work for much of a discount and in fact charge 4-10 times the price of wholesale contractors. Wholesale contractors are usually newer to the busines, they're willing to work with investors, and they charge very little. Some people thing that you will lose quality for working with them, but that is not necessarily true.

The 2 pitfalls: New investors who hire retail contractors end up paying far too much for rehab. This eats away profits and causes failure for most new investors. The other pitfall is high end finishes. If it is a luxury home, invest in high end touches. However most flips require the bare minimum quality product balanced with marketability. Doing a flip is not your chance to practice being an interior designer. Instead it's a change to practice discipline in keeping your costs low.

Step 4: Selling

- **Market Knowledge**: Understand the real estate market trends in your area. This will help in pricing the property correctly after renovation.

- **Real Estate Agent Partnership**: Partner with an experienced real estate agent who can effectively market and sell the property.

Step 5: Risk Management

- **Contingency Plans**: Have a plan for if the property doesn't sell quickly. This might include renting the property or refinancing.

- **Legal Considerations**: Ensure all legal and compliance aspects are in order, including permits and inspections.

BEWARE OF THE HAMSTER WHEEL

Fix and flips can be a dynamic and profitable entry point into the world of real estate, offering a way to build initial capital. However, it's important to recognize their place as just one phase in the broader journey towards sustained wealth creation. While engaging and potentially lucrative, fix and flips should not be viewed as the final destination but rather as a stepping stone. This is particularly relevant when considering the tax implications associated with this type of income.

Flipping houses is akin to a high-intensity job. It requires substantial time, effort, and skill, and though it can yield significant returns, these profits are typically subject to higher taxes compared to long-term investment income. The income generated from flipping is classified as active income and is taxed at regular income rates, which is significantly higher than the capital gains taxes on long-term investments. This tax burden impacts the net profit and should be a key consideration in your financial strategy.

Moreover, the income from flipping ceases when the work stops, unlike passive income streams which continue to generate revenue over time. This distinction highlights why flipping, while effective for capital accumulation, is not the optimal strategy for building lasting wealth. The real power of real estate investment lies in its ability to generate continuous, passive income and long-term capital appreciation. Friends I have who flip full-time, making well over a million in net income per year, are extremely busy and are failing to build lasting wealth, despite their high income. When the market turns the find themselves struggling to stay afloat. Don't make the same mistake they did.

In the next chapters, we will explore real estate investment methods that are more suited for creating generational wealth. These include strategies like owning rental properties, investing in commercial real estate, and other forms of long-term holdings. These methods not only provide a steady income stream but also come with the advantage of lower tax rates on long-term capital gains and potential tax deductions, making them more efficient in terms of wealth accumulation.

The transition from active real estate activities like flipping to more passive, long-term investment strategies is a crucial step for anyone aiming to build significant, lasting wealth. This evolution involves shifting focus from immediate, hands-on profit-making ventures to developing a portfolio of assets that provide stable, ongoing returns. The skills and experiences gained from flipping are invaluable in this transition, providing a robust foundation for informed decision-making in more sophisticated real estate investments.

As we move forward, remember that the goal is not to abandon flipping entirely but to utilize it as a powerful tool for capital generation. The key is to leverage the profits from these active real estate endeavors into investments that offer long-term financial growth, stability, and a more favorable tax structure, ultimately leading you towards greater financial freedom and the creation of enduring wealth.

PART 2: MULTIPLICATION & DIVERSIFICATION

THREE

WEALTH-BUILDING RENTAL PORTFOLIOS

Real estate investing is often perceived as a gateway to quick riches. TV and social media profiles are full with tales of overnight millionaires flipping houses and living the high life. However, the reality of real estate investing, particularly when it comes to building a substantial and sustainable rental portfolio, is far more grounded in patience, strategic planning, and a mindset focused on long-term gain rather than immediate gratification.

In my experience as a coach to a few dozen fix-and-flip investors across the United States, I frequently push my clients to the next level with a fundamental principle that bridges the gap between making money and building lasting wealth. While the allure of quick profits from flipping properties is undeniable, the true shift in your financial trajectory begins when you decide to hold a property rather than sell it.

After my coaching clients make their first $100,000 in profits with flips I encourage them to hold every other flip. After a few years the passive income builds momentum like an unstoppable freight train (much more efficiently than flipping) while also giving you your time back.

This approach demands a shift in mindset, from the quick wins of flipping to the patient accumulation of wealth through rentals. My advice to every investor is to find a balance: capitalize on the immediate gains from flipping, then transition to holding properties, aiming for a future rich in financial freedom. This path is not about the immediate payoff; it's about laying the groundwork for a life where financial security is not just a goal but a reality.

The essence of this strategy is twofold. First, there's the concept of cash flow— the immediate, tangible income from rental properties that can cover your bills and fund your vacations. It's the day-to-day financial fuel that provides stability and freedom in the present. However, while cash flow covers the now, the true wealth lies in the equity accumulated in the properties over time. As rents typically double every ten years, your monthly revenue could leap from $2,500 to $5,000, with the costs of holding the property rising at a much slower pace. This explosive increase in cash flow enhances your lifestyle, offering financial breathing space never before thought possible.

Yet, it's crucial to understand that the real, life-changing wealth comes from the equity built within these assets. Over time, as the property values increase and mortgage balances decrease, the equity — the difference between what your properties are worth and what you owe— grows exponentially. This equity is the cornerstone of long-term wealth, a financial bastion that ensures not just a comfortable life but a legacy.

In this chapter, we delve into how to strategically build a rental portfolio that not just sustains, but flourishes, providing both the cash flow to enjoy life now and the equity that secures your financial future. It's a holistic view of real estate investment, emphasizing that while cash flow allows for a life well-lived, the real wealth comes from the equity amassed through wise, long-term holdings.

Let this chapter guide you through the nuanced landscape of building wealth through real estate. It's about recognizing the immediate benefits of cash flow and the profound, enduring value of equity. Together, they form the dual paths to financial freedom, shaping not just how you live today but ensuring prosperity for years to come.

CHOOSE ONE: WEALTH OR IMMEDIATE REWARD

Real estate investment is not a sprint; it's a marathon. It's about laying a foundation that will stand the test of time, weather market fluctuations, and grow steadily. The key is to understand that this is not a get-rich-quick scheme. You are about to embark on a journey of building wealth through calculated decisions, informed risks, and a steadfast commitment to your long-term vision.

Consider this fundamental principle: true wealth in real estate is often a matter of delayed gratification. You will constantly have to choose between long term wealth or immediate reward. Choosing wealth is all about forgoing the quick buck today for a much larger return tomorrow. This approach may test your patience, especially when faced with seemingly lucrative short-term opportunities. However, the rewards of this approach, both financially and personally, are immense and enduring.

In real estate, particularly in appreciating markets, you may find that your rental income initially barely covers your mortgage payments, perhaps even dipping into negative cash flow. This scenario might seem counterintuitive to wealth building, but it's important to look at the bigger picture. Over time, as the property appreciates in value and rent prices increase, what was once a break-even investment can transform into a highly profitable one.

RENTAL PORTFOLIO STRATEGIES

HOUSEHACKING: A STEPPING STONE TO REAL ESTATE MASTERY

Househacking is often the starting point for many real estate investors. It’s a strategy that embodies both prudence and opportunity. By purchasing a multi-family property and living in one of the units while renting out the others, investors can significantly reduce or even eliminate their living expenses. This strategy isn’t just about saving money; it’s an invaluable learning experience, offering a hands-on introduction to property management and tenant relations without the full plunge into the landlord territory.

Real-Life Application: John's journey began with the purchase of a triplex in a burgeoning neighborhood. By living in one unit and renting out the other two, John was able to negate his mortgage and maintenance expenses. This setup allowed him not only to live rent-free but also to accumulate savings for his next investment venture.

It's a perfect example of how househacking can serve as a launchpad into the broader world of real estate investment.

LIVE-IN FLIPS: MAXIMIZING VALUE THROUGH RESIDENCE

Live-in flips represent a unique strategy in the real estate investment spectrum, blending the concept of a primary residence with the profitability of a flip. This approach involves purchasing a home, living in it while making improvements, and then selling it for a profit. The key advantage here is the potential tax benefit that comes from selling a primary residence, coupled with the value added through strategic updates.

One of the most compelling reasons to consider a live-in flip is the significant tax advantage it offers. According to current tax laws, if you live in your home for at least two of the five years preceding the sale, you may be exempt from capital gains tax on the profit up to a certain limit. This exemption can result in substantial savings, making live-in flips an attractive option for those looking to maximize their investment return.

PRO TIP 1: CHOOSING THE RIGHT PROPERTY

The success of a live-in flip largely depends on selecting the right property. Look for homes that are essentially move-in ready but somewhat outdated or in need of cosmetic updates. These properties are often priced below their potential market value, providing an opportunity to increase their worth through improvements.

PRO TIP 2: FINANCING THE RENOVATIONS

There are several ways to finance the updates on your live-in flip. You can use savings, or if you prefer not to dip into your reserves, consider a Home Equity Line of Credit (HELOC). A HELOC can be particularly useful in the latter part of your two-year residency, allowing you to complete the renovations and sell the home at an increased value.

PRO TIP 3: WORKING WITH REAL ESTATE PROFESSIONALS

Before embarking on renovations, consult with a local realtor to ensure the updates you're planning will indeed increase the property's value in your specific market. This step is crucial as it helps avoid overcapitalizing on improvements that don't yield a sufficient return on investment.

PRO TIP 4: TIMING THE MARKET

While living in the property, keep a close eye on market trends. If the market is favorable, listing the property after two years can maximize your profits. However, if the market experiences a downturn during your residence, it may be more prudent to extend your stay until market conditions improve. This flexibility is one of the live-in flip's advantages; if you need to wait out the market, you're doing so in an updated and comfortable home.

PRO TIP 5: DESIGN CONSIDERATIONS

When making updates, focus on changes that appeal to a broad range of buyers. Avoid overly personalized or bold design choices that might not resonate with the mainstream market. Neutral colors, quality fixtures, and universally appealing updates are usually safe bets. If your home is in a higher price bracket, consider engaging an interior designer to ensure that your updates align with current market trends and buyer preferences.

PRO TIP 6: A BALANCED APPROACH

Live-in flips require a balanced approach. On one hand, you're creating a home for yourself; on the other, you're strategically updating a property for profit. This balance is key to successfully navigating a live-in flip. By making smart renovation choices, staying informed about the market, and understanding the tax implications, you can enjoy the benefits of homeownership while building wealth through real estate.

In conclusion, live-in flips offer a unique opportunity to combine your living situation with a profitable investment strategy. By understanding and strategically navigating the nuances of property selection, renovation, market timing, and tax implications, you can successfully leverage this approach to enhance your real estate portfolio and overall financial wellbeing.

The live-in flip strategy, when integrated into a long-term real estate investment plan, can significantly amplify your wealth-building potential. The essence of this approach lies in its cyclical nature — rehab a property, benefit from tax savings upon selling after two years, and then reinvest the profits into the next project. This cycle can be repeated, each time scaling up your investments and expanding your real estate portfolio.

EXIT STRATEGY

After renovating your live-in flip and residing in it for the requisite two years to avail of the capital gains tax exemption, you can sell the property. The profit from this sale, exempt from significant taxes, represents a substantial capital gain. This profit can then serve as a down payment for a more expensive or larger property, allowing you to gradually move up the property ladder.

Each successive property can be more ambitious than the last, either in terms of size, location, or the scale of the renovation required. This upward trajectory not only enhances your living standards over time but also ensures that each project contributes to a growing investment portfolio.

An alternative to selling the property outright after two years is to convert it into a rental unit. This transition can be particularly advantageous if the property is in a high-demand area for rentals. By renting out the property, you establish a continuous income stream, which not only pays for the property's ongoing expenses but also generates profit.

Simultaneously, you can move on to your next live-in flip project, repeating the process of renovating and living in the new property for two years. This strategy effectively sets in motion a cycle of accumulating properties, each becoming a part of your rental portfolio after serving as your primary residence.

Once you've transitioned your renovated property into a rental and moved into a new home, consider a cash-out refinance on the rental property. This financial move allows you to tap into the equity you've built up, giving you a lump sum of cash that can be used to fund your next investment, whether it's another live-in flip or a different type of real estate venture.

This strategy optimizes your financial leverage, using the equity from one property to fuel the acquisition and renovation of the next. It's a powerful tool in accelerating your portfolio growth, allowing you to simultaneously own multiple properties and continuously work on new projects.

SHORT-TERM RENTALS: PLEASURE AND PROFIT

The advent of platforms like Airbnb has revolutionized the rental market, particularly in prime tourist destinations. Short-term rentals offer a unique opportunity for high rental yields and personal enjoyment. This strategy is particularly appealing for those who want to combine their investment with their lifestyle. By investing in properties located in areas you and your family love to visit, you create dual-purpose assets – personal retreats that also serve as income generators.

This approach to building a portfolio of short-term rental properties offers a unique blend of personal enjoyment and financial prudence, particularly when these properties are located in your favorite vacation spots. This strategy not only enhances your lifestyle but also stands as a niche long-term investment approach, weaving together the joy of vacationing with the practicality of real estate investment.

BUILDING A PORTFOLIO IN FAVORITE VACATION SPOTS

For many investors, the idea of owning properties in places they love to visit holds immense appeal. This approach transforms vacation destinations into assets, allowing you to enjoy these locales as a traveler while simultaneously reaping the benefits of property ownership. Over time, you can expand this portfolio, acquiring more properties in these areas, which not only diversifies your investment but also enriches your personal life.

ADVANTAGES OF FOCUSING ON A SINGLE VACATION AREA

If you and your family are fond of a particular vacation spot and visit it frequently, concentrating your property acquisitions in this area can be a wise strategy. This focused approach has several long-term benefits:

1. **Vendor Relationships:** By acquiring multiple properties in one area, you can build strong, long-lasting relationships with local vendors such as plumbers, electricians, handymen, and interior designers. Having a reliable network of service providers ensures efficient maintenance and management of your properties, enhancing their appeal and reducing the likelihood of extended downtimes.

2. **Streamlined Property Management:** Utilizing the same property management for all your properties in the area can streamline operations. A single property manager familiar with all your properties can manage them more effectively, ensuring consistency in guest experience and operational standards.

3. **Economies of Scale:** As your portfolio in the area grows, you can achieve economies of scale in property maintenance and management. Bulk deals with service providers or shared amenities across properties can reduce costs and increase your overall investment returns.

TAX BENEFITS OF VACATION-PROPERTY INVESTMENTS

One of the often-overlooked advantages of this strategy is the potential for tax deductions. When you visit your vacation properties, you can allocate a portion of your trip to inspecting and managing these investments. These visits, when documented properly, can be considered business trips, allowing you to deduct a significant portion of your travel expenses, including airfare, accommodation, and even dining, under the guise of property management and maintenance.

To maximize this benefit, it's crucial to maintain detailed records of the business activities carried out during these trips. Consult with a tax professional to ensure that your deductions are aligned with IRS guidelines and to understand the nuances of what can and cannot be deducted.

INCORPORATING THIS STRATEGY INTO YOUR INVESTMENT PORTFOLIO

When integrating short-term rental properties into your investment portfolio, consider the following steps:

1. **Research and Select:** Identify locations that you and your family enjoy and that also have strong potential for short-

term rental demand. Factors like tourist attractions, seasonality, and local rental regulations should be considered.

2. **Acquire Gradually:** Start with one property and understand the dynamics of the local short-term rental market. Once comfortable, gradually expand your portfolio in the area.

3. **Optimize and Scale:** Use your experiences from each property to optimize your operations. Apply these learnings to new acquisitions, ensuring each new property benefits from past insights.

4. **Professional Management:** Even if you are familiar with the area, employing a professional property management service can greatly reduce the burden of day-to-day operations, allowing you to focus on strategic growth.

5. **Regular Visits and Maintenance:** Plan regular visits to your properties, combining business with pleasure. Use these trips to inspect your properties, meet with your local team, and enjoy your vacation.

6. **Tax Planning:** Work with a tax advisor to understand how you can leverage tax deductions related to your property inspections and management activities during your vacations.

By following this strategy, you not only create a portfolio of lucrative short-term rental properties but also enrich your personal life with enjoyable vacation experiences, all while building significant long-term wealth.

ACQUISITION STRATEGIES

Acquiring real estate properties can be a complex process, especially when traditional financing methods aren't feasible or optimal for your investment strategy. Fortunately, there are several alternative acquisition strategies that savvy investors use to facilitate property purchases. These methods not only offer flexibility in financing but also can provide unique advantages in the right circumstances. Let’s explore some of these creative acquisition strategies, including seller financing, subject to existing financing, wrap around mortgages, wholesaling, and private money.

SELLER FINANCING: CUSTOMIZED FINANCING SOLUTIONS

Seller financing, often referred to as owner financing, is a method where the seller of the property takes on the role of the lender. Instead of paying the full price upfront, the buyer makes payments to the seller over a period of time, as per the terms agreed upon in the financing agreement.

- **Flexibility**: This method can offer more flexible terms than traditional bank loans, including potentially lower down payments and customizable repayment schedules.

- **Benefits for Buyers and Sellers**: Buyers who might not qualify for conventional loans find this method advantageous, while sellers benefit by making their property more attractive to a broader range of buyers. Additionally, sellers can earn interest on the loan, often at a higher rate than traditional investments.

SUBJECT-TO EXISTING FINANCING

Acquiring a property 'subject to' existing financing means that you purchase the property but the existing mortgage remains in place. The buyer agrees to take over the mortgage payments, but the loan itself stays in the original borrower's name.

- **Advantages**: This strategy can be beneficial if the existing mortgage has favorable terms, such as a low-interest rate. It also reduces the amount of capital the buyer needs to enter the deal, making it an attractive option for those with limited upfront cash.

- **Legal Considerations**: It's crucial to handle these transactions carefully, as they can involve complex legal and financial considerations. Proper documentation and understanding of the risks involved are essential.

WRAP AROUND MORTGAGES: COMPLEX BUT REWARDING

A wrap around mortgage is a type of loan where a new mortgage is created to encompass the existing one. The new mortgage 'wraps around' the existing debt.

- **Flexibility in Financing**: This method can offer flexibility in terms of financing, particularly when it comes to negotiating interest rates and down payments.

- **Risks and Rewards**: While wrap around mortgages can provide creative solutions for financing, they come with their complexities and legal intricacies. Both parties should be aware of the risks and benefits involved, and it's often advisable to involve legal counsel in these transactions.

WHOLESALING: QUICK TURNAROUND DEALS

Wholesaling in real estate involves entering into a contract to purchase a property and then assigning that contract to another buyer for a higher price before the original contract closes.

- **No Need for Financing**: This strategy is unique in that it doesn't typically require the wholesaler to actually purchase the property or secure financing. Instead, the wholesaler earns a profit from the contract assignment fee.

- **Fast Profits**: Wholesaling can be a quick way to earn money in real estate without significant capital, though it requires a deep understanding of market values and strong negotiation skills.

PRIVATE MONEY: PERSONALIZED LOAN AGREEMENTS

Private money refers to loans from private individuals or entities, as opposed to traditional financial institutions. These can be friends, family, or private investors looking to earn interest on their money through real estate deals.

- **Tailored Terms**: Terms of private money loans are negotiable and can be tailored to suit the specific needs of the investor and the lender.

- **Building Relationships**: Utilizing private money often involves building strong relationships with lenders and demonstrating a reliable track record as an investor.

TURN-KEY RENTAL PROPERTIES

While building your portfolio you'll inevitably be tempted by the easy option of purchasing turn key rental properties. These properties are often marketed as hassle-free investments, ready for immediate rental with little to no need for renovations or updates. While they might seem alluring, especially to those seeking quick cash flow and minimal involvement, it's crucial to zoom out and view the bigger picture, particularly in the context of long-term wealth building.

THE ALLURE OF IMMEDIATE REWARD VS. LONG-TERM EQUITY GROWTH

Turn key rental properties often promise immediate rental income, appealing to investors looking for a quick start in the rental market. However, this immediate reward can sometimes come at the cost of long-term wealth accumulation. Here's why:

1. **Lack of Appreciation**: Many turn key properties are located in markets that don't experience significant appreciation. While they can provide steady cash flow, they may not significantly increase in value over time, limiting your potential for long-term wealth growth.

2. **Missed Opportunities to Force Equity**: One of the most effective ways to rapidly increase a property's value is through strategic renovations and updates, a concept known as "forcing equity." Turn key properties, already refurbished and rent-ready, offer little to no opportunity for this kind of value addition.

THE RULE OF THUMB: APPROACH WITH CAUTION

Given these considerations, here’s a rule of thumb for investors focusing on building lasting wealth: be wary of turn key rental systems. While not all turn key properties are poor investments, many are not situated in appreciating markets and don't offer the opportunity to force equity. This can result in a scenario where you're earning rental income but not significantly growing your investment's value over time.

CONSIDERATIONS FOR TURN KEY PROPERTY INVESTMENTS:

1. **Market Research**: Before investing in a turn key property, thoroughly research the market. Look for areas with strong indicators of growth and appreciation.

2. **Value-Adding Potential**: Evaluate if there's any scope to add value to the property in the future. Even minor renovations could lead to significant increases in property value.

3. **Weighing Cash Flow vs. Equity**: Consider your investment goals. If immediate cash flow is a priority and you're less concerned about long-term appreciation, a turn key property might be suitable. However, if your goal is substantial wealth

accumulation, focusing on properties with potential for equity growth is advisable.

4. **Diversification**: If you opt for a turn key property, consider balancing your portfolio with other properties that offer stronger potential for appreciation and value addition.

BUILDING A RENTAL PORTFOLIO

No matter what you do to acquire the properties, building a rental property portfolio worth over $20,000,000 over the next 20 years is not some far out dream, but a highly achievable goal. By methodically adding one property each year to your portfolio, you're not just collecting assets; you're cultivating a garden of opportunities that flourish in value and consistently bear the fruit of cash flow. This strategy is particularly viable if you have a consistent source of high income, allowing you to reliably set aside enough for annual down payments.

The cornerstone of this endeavor lies in targeting real estate markets on the rise and properties that guarantee a steady flow of rental income. Zones buzzing with job growth, population surges, and infrastructure developments are your gold mines. These areas typically see properties appreciating at a healthy pace. Parallelly, zeroing in on properties that attract long-term tenants ensures a stable income stream to fuel further investments and comfortably cover your operational costs. Each property you choose is a calculated step towards risk mitigation and maximized returns.

Aim for properties nestled in high-income neighborhoods or near coveted amenities, like newly opened elementary schools. Such locations are magnets for higher-paying tenants and offer greater rental stability. They often experience a stronger demand for rentals, translating to shorter vacancy periods and the potential for more competitive rental rates. Year after year, as you carefully handpick and add new properties in these sought-after areas to your portfolio, you're likely to witness not just a steady but an increasing flow of rental income, positively impacting your overall cash flow. Furthermore, these properties are usually more insulated against market downturns, safeguarding their long-term value.

Envision starting with an initial property valued at around $500,000, which means bringing about $100,000 to the table for the down payment. In the following year, you repeat this process. But what about the monthly cash flow from these properties? The strategy here is to use it to chip away at the mortgage principal, starting with the property that has the smallest balance remaining.

Here’s a realistic picture: each property in your portfolio aligns with the average market price, appreciates by 5% annually, and experiences a 3% yearly increase in rent. With these factors at play, each property in your portfolio is poised to reach an estimated value of around $1 million in 20 years. Consequently, your collection of 20 homes would be valued at over $20 million. By diligently using the cash flow to pay down the mortgage principal, you could be looking at a portfolio with minimal to no debt by then. By time they’re all paid off, you can live off of the cashflow for the remainder of your retirement and still have a valuable real estate portfolio to pass on..

The essence of this strategy is rooted in consistency, strategic acquisitions, and focusing on quality over quantity. By the end of two decades, you'll have built not just a portfolio but something significant that passively supports your financial independence and delivers robust returns.

THE MOST POWERFUL WAY TO BUILD A RENTAL PORTFOLIO

Put on your seatbelt because things are about to get real wild. Are you ready? I'm about to introduce you to the single most powerful way to build wealth through residential real estate. And just to warn you, when you double check my math on this you'll see that my numbers are at the conservative end of the spectrum. Later in the book I will teach you even more powerful ways to build wealth even faster, but this is where we really start to get some traction.

The BRRRR method, based on the book by David Mason Greene – Buy, Rehab, Rent, Refinance, Repeat – is an approach that, when followed diligently, can lead to substantial growth of your residential rental portfolio. This strategy revolves around the idea of recycling your capital. You start by purchasing undervalued properties, often those that require some level of renovation. By rehabilitating these properties, you not only enhance their value but also their rental appeal. Once these properties are rented out and generating income, you can refinance them based on their increased value, freeing up capital to reinvest in your next project.

The BRRRR strategy's power lies in its ability to multiply an initial investment into a vast portfolio over time. Let's break down how starting with a single property and a modest initial investment can lead to substantial wealth accumulation.

THE SEED OF INVESTMENT

Imagine you begin with your first BRRRR property, a modest investment of $150,000. You bring in $30,000 for the down payment and another $20,000 for rehab and closing costs, totaling an initial investment of $50,000. Once this property is rehabbed, rented, and then refinanced, you get most, if not all, of your initial investment back. This cash is then ready to be reinvested into your next BRRRR property.

EXPONENTIAL GROWTH THROUGH REINVESTMENT

With the capital from the first refinance in hand, you purchase two more properties the next year. As your experience and systems improve, you double your acquisitions each subsequent year: four properties the next year, then eight, and so on. This exponential growth model is feasible due to the recycling of the same initial capital through the BRRRR process and streamlined systems.

PROJECTED GROWTH OVER 20 YEARS

Assuming you continue this pace, and cap it at one new rental per month by year 5, let's project the growth over 20 years:

- Year 1: 1 property

- Year 2: 2 properties

Year 3: 4 properties

- Year 4: 8 properties
- Year 5: 12 properties (one property per month for now on)
- And Eventually Year 20: 195 properties

By this model, by year 20, you could potentially accumulate around 195 properties. The average home value today in the US is about $500,000, which would mean that your portfolio's value would be approximately $97,500,000. However, this calculation does not take into consideration how homes tend to raise in value over time. The average has been more than 8% over the last 50 years. This puts the value of your portfolio in 20 years at closer to $220,000,000. Lastly this calculation is not taking into consideration rent checks you would have collected net positive over the 20 year term. Let's continue to dive into this math.

CASH FLOW AND APPRECIATION

Let's make the safe assumption that you cashflow about $500 per month per property. Rent rates across the board tend to increase by 3% per year (Even more in appreciating markets). At year 20, you will be cashflowing about $140,000 per month. That's $1.68 million per year in passive income cashflow. In appreciating markets, with an average appreciation rate of over 5% per year, your portfolio's total value will likely be worth over $220 million by then. These are conservative estimates; in reality, appreciation rates are usually significantly higher, and rent increases much more in appreciating markets.

One of the most powerful tools of real estate investing is depreciation. We will unpack this in greater detail in chapter 8. But here's an example of its power in effect. Over the 20 years of building this BRRRR rental portfolio, you could depreciate almost $10,000,000 in property value, starting with approximately $90,000 in just the second year. This depreciation can significantly reduce your tax burden each year from income tax, effectively lowering your taxable income while you build lasting wealth. Therefore your overall gain will be much higher than described in your rental portfolio.

It's important to engage in strategic tax planning throughout this process. The ability to offset income through depreciation, coupled with the tax advantages of property ownership, can lead to substantial tax savings, further enhancing the profitability of your investments.

Multiplication

The essence of the BRRRR strategy's effectiveness lies in its ability to generate substantial growth from a single initial investment. To clarify, the exponential growth of your real estate portfolio, as outlined previously, can potentially be achieved with nothing more than the original $50,000 invested in your first property. This initial capital sets the foundation for a self-perpetuating cycle of investment that continues to grow over time, with no need for additional out-of-pocket investment.

Consider the scenario where you begin with $50,000, allocated as a down payment and rehabilitation costs for your first BRRRR property. Once this property is renovated, rented out, and refinanced, the key is that the refinancing step typically allows you to pull out most of this initial investment. This recaptured capital is then ready to be funneled into acquiring your next property.

As you continue to apply the BRRRR strategy to each subsequent property, the initial $50,000 essentially gets recycled over and over. Each refinancing phase after rehab and renting is designed to recoup your investment, which you then use to fund the next purchase and rehab. This method means that, after the initial property, you are not pulling more money from your pocket; instead, you are using the recycled capital from your ongoing real estate transactions.

GROWTH WITHOUT ADDITIONAL OUT-OF-POCKET EXPENSES

This cycle leads to a snowball effect. With each successful BRRRR cycle, your portfolio grows without the need for additional personal funds. Your initial $50,000 investment continues to work for you, moving from one property to the next.

- Year 1: Your journey starts with one property and your $50,000 investment.

- Year 2 and Beyond: With each subsequent year, as you reinvest the recaptured capital, your property count increases exponentially, yet your personal financial contribution remains capped at the original $50,000.

THE IMPACT OF GROWTH OVER TIME

Over the course of 20 years, following this method, you build a substantial portfolio, as projected previously, with around 218 properties, assuming continuous reinvestment and no additional personal financial input after the initial investment. The cash flow and property value appreciation only add to the wealth accumulated, all stemming from the original $50,000.

Conclusion

As we close the chapter on these foundational strategies for building a rental portfolio, it's clear now that real estate has the capacity to compound exponentially with time. From the smart beginnings of househacking to the clever maneuvers of live-in flips, and the transformative power of the BRRRR method, each strategy you've seen here lays another brick in the fortress of your future financial independence.

But, as captivating as these strategies are, they merely scratch the surface of what's possible in the world of real estate investment. What if I told you that the next chapter holds the keys to even greater realms of wealth? That we're about to delve into secret tools and strategies that the wealthiest real estate tycoons have used to build their empires? Strategies so powerful, they transform the ambitious into the accomplished, the dreamers into the doers.

In the upcoming chapters, we pull back the curtain to reveal these secret tools - the ones used by billionaires to exponentially grow their portfolios. We're not just talking about making money; we're talking about creating a legacy. A legacy that not only secures your financial future but also paves the way for generations to come.

So, as you turn these pages, prepare to be immersed in deeper insights, game-changing tactics, and the kind of knowledge that could skyrocket your journey from real estate enthusiast to mogul. Get ready to learn, adapt, and apply the secret tools of the wealthiest real estate investors – because your path to extraordinary wealth begins now.

FOUR

NON-NEGOTIABLES

As you turn the pages of this chapter, you're not just reading another segment of a book; you're learning the hidden secrets of some of the biggest real estate portfolio managers in the world. This chapter isn't about quick wins or overnight success; it's about the art of crafting a legacy, one property at a time. In the world of real estate, time is more than just a ticking clock; it's an invaluable asset, a currency that can buy you freedom, growth, and ultimately, a life of fulfillment. Here, we dive deep into the vital elements that make or break the journey of portfolio building – understanding the true worth of your time, mastering the art of market research, and tracking your progress with precision.

This journey is akin to navigating a vast ocean. Your properties are the ships, and your strategies and plans are the compass and map guiding you to treasure-laden shores. As Steve Jobs wisely put it, "People overestimate what they can do in a year and underestimate what they can do in a decade." This chapter is about thinking big, planning meticulously, and executing consistently. It's about setting a course for decades, not just years, and recognizing that every step, no matter how small, moves you closer to your grand vision.

In these pages, you'll learn to value your time like the rarest diamond, explore markets with the keen eye of a seasoned explorer, and track your progress with the precision of a master architect. This isn't just about building wealth; it's about building a future that echoes through generations.

VALUE YOUR TIME: USE A PROPERTY MANAGEMENT COMPANY

One of the most compelling reasons to engage property management companies is the value of your time. As an investor, your primary goal is to grow your portfolio and accumulate wealth, which requires strategic thinking, market research, and networking. Managing properties, especially as your portfolio expands, can become a full-time job in itself, consuming the time and energy that could be better spent on high-value activities like identifying new investment opportunities or planning portfolio expansion.

- **Cost vs. Benefit**: Property management fees, often a percentage of the rental income, might seem like an added expense, but they should be viewed in light of the value they bring. These fees are modest compared to the time and effort they save, which can be redirected towards activities that significantly enhance your portfolio's value.

- **Efficiency and Expertise**: Property managers bring efficiency and expertise to the day-to-day operations of rental properties. From tenant screening to maintenance, from rent collection to handling legal issues, their professional management ensures that your properties are well-maintained and profitable.

LEVERAGING TIME FOR PORTFOLIO GROWTH

Your time as an investor is best spent on tasks that leverage the growth of your portfolio. This includes exploring new markets, building networks, securing financing for future purchases, and staying abreast of industry trends and regulations.

- **Opportunity Cost**: Every hour spent on property management is an hour lost that could have been used in seeking new investment opportunities or devising strategies for portfolio growth. The opportunity cost of self-management can often outweigh the cost of hiring a property management company.

- **Scaling Your Investments**: As your portfolio grows, the complexity and demands of property management increase exponentially. Property management companies allow you to scale your investments without being bogged down by the increasing operational workload.

LONG-TERM STRATEGIC FOCUS

Employing a property management company aligns with a long-term strategic focus in real estate investing. It's about building a business system that works efficiently, where your role is to steer the ship rather than manning every oar.

•

Focus on High-Value Decisions: Freeing yourself from day-to-day management allows you to focus on high-value decisions that affect the long-term success and growth of your investments.

- **Sustainable Investing**: With property managers handling the operational aspects, your investing becomes more sustainable. It prevents burnout and keeps you focused on your long-term financial goals.

In essence, leveraging the services of property management companies is a strategic decision that aligns with the core objectives of real estate investing. It's not just about delegating tasks; it's about optimizing your role as an investor to focus on growth, strategy, and wealth accumulation. Your time is indeed worth more than a property management fee, and recognizing this is key to building a successful and scalable real estate portfolio.

TARGET YOUR MARKET:

Market research is a critical component of successful real estate investing. It involves a strategic approach to selecting markets that are not only profitable but also align with your investment goals and risk tolerance. Here's how to conduct thorough market research to identify the ideal location for your investments.

1. PRIORITIZE LANDLORD-FRIENDLY STATES

Firstly, focus on states with laws that favor landlords. These areas typically have quicker and more efficient processes for dealing with tenant issues like non-payment or eviction. Landlord-friendly states often provide a more stable and predictable environment for real estate investment, reducing potential legal hassles and uncertainties.

2. IDENTIFY EMERGING MARKETS

Look for regions experiencing a net influx of people. A growing population usually indicates a vibrant, expanding economy, which can lead to increased demand for housing. This growth can be a result of various factors like job opportunities, quality of life, and economic development. An emerging market with more people moving in than out is likely to have a robust rental market.

3. FOCUS ON AREAS WITH HOUSING SHORTAGES

Markets with housing shortages present a significant opportunity for landlords. In these areas, the demand for rental properties often outstrips supply, potentially leading to higher rental rates and lower vacancy rates. However, be mindful of local regulations or developments that might be aimed at addressing these shortages.

4. CONSIDER LONG-TERM GROWTH POTENTIAL

Invest in markets that show promise for sustained growth over the coming decades. Research factors like economic diversification, infrastructural development plans, and demographic trends. Markets with a strong foundation for continued growth are more likely to offer long-term stability and profitability for your investments.

5. CHOOSE A FAMILIAR MARKET OR ONE YOU CAN MONITOR

Invest in a market that you know well or have the capacity to keep up with. Familiarity with the local area, its neighborhoods, and trends can give you an edge in making informed decisions. If you're investing in an unfamiliar market, ensure you have reliable sources of information and local contacts.

6. IDENTIFY THE AVERAGE HOME PRICE

The average home price in your target market serves as a benchmark for your investments. It gives you a clear idea of the typical property value in the area, helping you make informed decisions about which properties fall within a reasonable price range.

Staying Within 15% of the Average: Aim to invest in properties that when fully updated are within 15% of the market's average home price. This range is strategic for several reasons:

- **Lower End Caution**: Properties significantly below the average price might seem like bargains, but they often come with hidden costs. These might include higher maintenance expenses, difficulties in attracting and retaining reliable tenants, and potentially lower property appreciation.

- **Upper End Caution**: Conversely, properties priced well above the average can pose risks as well. These might be harder to rent due to their higher price point, and you could face longer vacancy periods, which can impact your cash flow.

7. DEFINE YOUR BUY BOX

Your "Buy Box" is a set of criteria defining the ideal property you are looking to invest in. This includes property type, price range, location within the city, and other specific features important to you. Having a well-defined Buy Box helps you stay focused and makes it easier to communicate your investment criteria to others, such as real estate agents or wholesalers.

8. COLLABORATE WITH WHOLESALERS & REALTORS

Once you have defined your Buy Box, connect with wholesalers in your target area. They can be invaluable in finding deals that match your specifications. By clearly communicating your Buy Box to them, you ensure that you are presented with opportunities that align with your investment strategy.

Effective market research in real estate is about more than just understanding broad trends; it's about identifying specific opportunities that align with your investment goals and criteria. By focusing on landlord-friendly states, emerging markets with housing shortages, and areas with long-term growth potential, and by clearly defining your Buy Box, you set the stage for a successful real estate investment journey. Remember, the more targeted and informed your market research, the better positioned you are to make profitable investment decisions.

TRACK YOUR PROGRESS: SREO

There are several tools you will learn along the way, but the most crucial tool for you to implement from day one is the SREO, or Schedule of Real Estate Owned. This document is essential for investors who are actively managing and growing their property portfolios. Let's delve into what an SREO is, its purpose, and how to maintain and utilize it effectively as you build your real estate portfolio.

WHAT IS AN SREO?

An SREO is essentially a comprehensive list or spreadsheet that details all the real estate properties an individual or entity owns. It's a snapshot of your current real estate holdings and their respective financial statuses. This document is often required by lenders when you apply for loans, especially as your portfolio grows, to assess your financial health and real estate experience.

COMPONENTS OF AN SREO

A typical SREO includes the following information for each property:

1. **Property Address**: The full address of each property.

2. **Property Type**: Whether it's a single-family home, multi-family unit, commercial property, etc.

3. **Date Purchased**: When the property was acquired.

4. **Purchase Price**: The amount paid to acquire the property.

Current Market Value: An estimate of the property's value in the current market.

6. **Mortgage Lender Information**: Details of the lender if the property is mortgaged.
7. **Loan Amount**: Original loan amount for the property.
8. **Current Loan Balance**: The remaining amount of the loan.
9. **Monthly Mortgage Payment**: The amount paid monthly for the mortgage.
10. **Rental Income**: The income generated monthly from the property.
11. **Operating Expenses**: Regular expenses incurred in the maintenance and management of the property.
12. **Net Operating Income**: The income left after all operating expenses are paid.

PURPOSE AND USES OF AN SREO

1. **Loan Applications**: When applying for new loans or refinancing, lenders will often request your SREO to assess your financial stability and real estate management skills.
2. **Portfolio Analysis and Management**: Regularly updating your SREO helps in analyzing the performance of your

properties, identifying which are profitable and which may be underperforming.

3. **Strategic Planning**: It aids in making informed decisions about future purchases, sales, or renovations based on the overall health of your portfolio

LEVERAGING AN SREO FOR WEALTH BUILDING

As you embark on your journey of building wealth through real estate, your SREO will be a vital tool for tracking your progress, understanding your financial standing, and planning for future growth. It offers a clear and organized view of your real estate investments, helping you make informed and strategic decisions. By effectively managing and utilizing your SREO, you position yourself for successful and scalable growth in the real estate domain as you begin to build life-changing generational wealth.

PROTECT YOUR ASSETS: NON-RECOURSE PORTFOLIO LOANS

When you have accumulated a substantial portfolio of 10-20 properties, do not forget to make this change. Refinance all of your properties into a blanket non-recourse portfolio loan. This strategy becomes particularly relevant and beneficial as your portfolio grows in size and value. Feel free to cash out some of the loan if you want. Use the cash on a dream vacation and the remainder on other real estate investments.

A non-recourse portfolio loan is a type of lending where the loan is secured by the portfolio of properties as collateral, but the lender's ability to recover the loan is limited to the collateral itself. In other words, in the event of a default, the lender can only seize the properties securing the loan and cannot pursue the borrower's other assets or personal income. This means that in a market downturn and or a lawsuit, your personal home and assets are safe from recourse. For the first 10 properties, your loans will all be recourse loans which holds a certain risk to your personal assets.

BENEFITS OF SWITCHING TO A NON-RECOURSE PORTFOLIO LOAN

1. **Risk Mitigation:** The most significant benefit of a non-recourse loan is the limited personal liability. In a worst-case scenario, your personal assets are protected from seizure, as the lender can only claim the properties tied to the loan.

2. **Easier Management of Multiple Properties:** Managing multiple individual mortgages can be complex and time-consuming. A non-recourse portfolio loan consolidates these mortgages into a single loan, simplifying the management and tracking of your financial obligations.

3. **Potential for Better Loan Terms:** When you consolidate multiple properties into a single loan, you may be able to negotiate better terms with lenders. This could include lower interest rates, longer amortization periods, or more favorable loan conditions, which can improve cash flow and profitability.

4.

Flexibility for Future Investments: A non-recourse portfolio loan can provide more flexibility in managing your portfolio. It can free up equity that can be used for further investments or restructuring your portfolio without affecting your personal credit or asset base.

5. **Tax Efficiency:** Consolidating loans and managing a large portfolio under a single loan structure can offer tax efficiencies. The interest on these loans is typically tax-deductible, and managing a single loan may reduce administrative costs and complexities.

6. **Scaling the Portfolio:** For investors looking to scale their portfolios further, a non-recourse portfolio loan can be an effective tool. It demonstrates to lenders and investors your commitment and capability to manage a significant portfolio, potentially opening doors for additional financing options.

CONSIDERATIONS BEFORE CONVERTING TO A NON-RECOURSE LOAN

- **Eligibility and Requirements:** Not all investors may qualify for a non-recourse loan. Lenders typically have stringent requirements regarding the portfolio's value, income generation, and the borrower's investment experience.

- **Costs and Fees:** There may be additional costs and fees associated with securing a non-recourse loan, including appraisal fees, legal fees, and potential prepayment penalties on existing mortgages.

-

Interest Rates and Terms: Carefully compare the interest rates and terms of a non-recourse loan against your current mortgages to ensure it is financially beneficial.

For real estate investors with a substantial portfolio, transitioning to a non-recourse portfolio loan offers a strategic way to manage risk, simplify portfolio management, and potentially secure better financing terms. It's a significant step in professionalizing your real estate investment operations, aligning with goals for portfolio expansion, and protecting personal assets. As with any major financial decision, it's advisable to consult with financial advisors and lending professionals to thoroughly understand the implications and benefits of this transition.

DEFINE YOUR GOALS

Pay attention to where you are at right now. You are at the brink of a decades-long journey, one that transforms not just your financial landscape but the very essence of your lifestyle and aspirations and future generations. This is where your boldest dreams are not just fanciful wishes, but blueprints for an actually attainable future. Steve Jobs once astutely observed, "People overestimate what they can do in a year and underestimate what they can do in a decade." In the world of property investment, this sentiment is a beacon of truth, illuminating the profound potential that lies in the long game. As you embark on this journey, it's not just about accumulating wealth or properties; it's about crafting a legacy, shaping a future that resonates with your deepest aspirations, and methodically charting the course to bring those visions to life.

DREAMING BIG AND REVERSE ENGINEERING

1. **Visualizing the Future**: Begin by imagining where you want to be in 20 years. Think expansively and boldly about your aspirations, not just in terms of wealth and assets, but also the lifestyle, experiences, and personal achievements you desire. This is your dream, unbound by current constraints or perceptions.

2. **Reverse Engineering Your Dreams**: With your long-term vision in mind, start breaking down these dreams into concrete goals. What does it take to realize these aspirations? If your vision includes a significant real estate portfolio, consider what it means in terms of the number of properties, their locations, and the income they should generate.

3. **Yearly Milestones**: Translate these overarching goals into annual objectives. What do you need to achieve each year to be on track towards your 20-year vision? This might involve acquiring a certain number of properties, reaching specific income targets, or developing key skills and networks.

MONTHLY COMMITMENTS AND RHYTHMS

- **Monthly Rythms**: Determine what routines you need to take every month to meet your yearly goals. This could include saving a certain amount for down payments, researching potential markets, networking with real estate professionals, or enhancing your knowledge about the next phase of investing that you plan to enter.

Weekly Actions: Establish regular habits and actions that align with your goals. Consistency in actions, whether it's monthly budgeting, attending real estate seminars, or reviewing market trends, is key to making steady progress.

THE NECESSITY OF A PLAN AND CONSISTENCY

- **The Roadmap**: Without a clear plan, your journey lacks direction and purpose. A well-thought-out plan acts as a roadmap, guiding your decisions and actions. It provides structure to your ambitions, turning lofty dreams into achievable goals.

- **The Power of Consistency**: Consistency is the fuel that propels you forward. It's easy to get distracted or discouraged, especially in a venture spanning two decades. Regular, consistent actions build momentum, helping you overcome challenges and stay focused on your long-term objectives.

What will happen over 20 years is both exhilarating and demanding. It requires not just dreaming big but also planning and consistently executing those plans. Remember, your future is shaped not by the dreams you have but by the daily actions you take. It will be hard work and it will be worth it. Each day, each decision, each investment brings you a step closer to the future you envision. Like a train it starts off slowly but eventually it builds momentum and force, your dream will become unstopable. With a clear plan in place and a commitment to consistent action, there's no limit to what you can achieve in the span of the coming decades.

FIVE

SURVEY OF NICHE PORTFOLIOS

Cultivating generational wealth happens with two overarching strategies: real estate investment and business ownership. This chapter combines these two, introducing you to niche real estate sectors that often blend the principles of property investment with the nuances of running a business. While subsequent chapters will focus intensively on our most recommended strategy, here we'll explore a variety of unique investment opportunities.

From the dependable cash flow of storage facilities to the dynamic operations of RV parks, each section is crafted to broaden your understanding and spark your interest in these lesser-known markets. These niches aren't just about buying and holding property; they're about uncovering potential, understanding market needs, and sometimes, managing an operational business intertwined with your investment. This chapter is your gateway to exploring how diverse real estate ventures can lay a solid foundation for long-term, generational wealth. Let's embark on this exploration, equipping you with insights and ideas to identify which of these unique opportunities aligns best with your vision for wealth creation.

STORAGE FACILITIES:

Storage facilities have become increasingly popular among investors over the past three years, with their demand and value steadily rising. This trend has led to a more competitive market, often resulting in premium prices for entry. Despite this, the investment can be highly worthwhile due to their recession resilience and potential for steady income.

GROWING INTEREST AND MARKET COMPETITION

In recent years, the storage facility market has seen a notable increase in investor interest. This surge is attributed to their proven performance during economic downturns, as people often downsize or seek storage during challenging times. As a result, investors might find themselves paying above traditional market rates to acquire these properties.

RECESSION RESILIENCE: A KEY ATTRACTION

One of the most compelling aspects of storage facilities is their resilience during economic downturns. Unlike other real estate sectors that might suffer during a recession, storage facilities often maintain steady occupancy rates. This resilience makes them an attractive option for investors looking for stable, long-term investments.

INVESTMENT STRATEGIES FOR STORAGE FACILITIES

-

Capitalize on Volume: With storage facilities, the game is about volume. Consider investing in expanding existing facilities to maximize rental space. Adding more units to your property can significantly increase your revenue potential.

- **Embrace Automation:** Investing in technology is crucial. Implement electronic entry gates, electronic locks, and automated billing and marketing systems. These upgrades not only reduce labor costs but also enhance the customer experience, making your facility more competitive.

- **Focus on Strategic Locations:** Given the increased competition, selecting the right location is more critical than ever. Look for areas with growing populations or limited storage options to ensure high demand.

OFFICE BUILDINGS:

THE STRATEGIC ADVANTAGE

Office buildings, especially in emerging business hubs or areas of corporate growth, can be a substantial income source. These properties often attract long-term leases, providing stable and predictable cash flow. The inclusion of office buildings in your portfolio can balance out the volatility of other investments, offering a hedge against market fluctuations.

LOCATION AND QUALITY TENANTS

Location is paramount in office real estate. Properties in central business districts or near transportation hubs are more likely to attract and retain high-quality tenants. However, beware of properties that seem undervalued for their location – they might be in areas with dwindling commercial activity or poor accessibility, which can lead to longer vacancy periods and lower returns.

LONG-TERM LEASING STRATEGY

Focusing on long-term leases with credible tenants can stabilize your income and reduce turnover costs. By offering competitive amenities and flexible lease terms, you can attract a diverse range of tenants, from burgeoning startups to established corporations, thereby diversifying your risk.

RETAIL BUILDINGS:

BALANCING RISK AND REWARD

Retail properties can offer high rewards, but the risks are also significant, especially in the age of e-commerce. A well-located retail property in a high-traffic area can yield substantial returns. However, properties in less desirable locations, or those dependent on a single tenant, can pose higher risks, especially if consumer shopping habits shift.

IMPORTANCE OF HIGH FOOT TRAFFIC

The success of retail properties largely hinges on their location. Prime locations with high visibility and foot traffic, such as those near anchor stores or in busy shopping districts, are more likely to succeed. Be cautious of lower-priced retail spaces in less frequented areas, as they may struggle to attract and retain tenants.

ADAPTING TO MARKET CHANGES

Investing in adaptable spaces is key. The ability to modify and repurpose spaces to suit various retail formats can make your property more attractive to tenants, especially as retail trends evolve. This adaptability can be a significant asset in maintaining high occupancy rates.

INDUSTRIAL PROPERTIES:

CONSISTENT DEMAND

Industrial properties, particularly in growing cities, are in consistent demand due to their role in commerce and manufacturing. As cities expand, the need for warehouses, distribution centers, and manufacturing facilities grows, providing a strong market for these types of properties.

MARKET ANALYSIS FOR LONG-TERM GROWTH

Conducting thorough market analysis is critical in industrial real estate investment. It's essential to identify areas with potential for long-term growth that will support and sustain tenants over time. Investing in industrial properties in rapidly developing areas can ensure a consistent demand for your space.

MODERN FACILITIES AND TENANT NEEDS

Prioritizing modern facilities that meet tenant needs is crucial. Tenants look for properties with features like high ceilings, large loading docks, and efficient layouts to facilitate their operations. Up-to-date facilities are more attractive and tend to secure longer leases.

HOTELS:

HIGH-RISK, HIGH-REWARD DYNAMIC

Hotel investments, especially in prime locations, can offer substantial returns. For example, luxury hotels in high-demand areas such as Manhattan have the potential for impressive Average Daily Rates (ADRs), sometimes exceeding $500. However, this high-reward potential is matched with equally high risks and operational demands.

CONSIDERATION: OPERATIONAL INTENSITY AND COSTS

Operating a hotel requires constant attention and significant labor, which can be costly and time-consuming. Hotels necessitate 24/7 customer service and operational management, making them a demanding investment in terms of both time and resources. The hospitality industry is also known for its high customer service expectations, adding another layer of operational complexity.

MARKET RESEARCH AND MANAGEMENT PARTNERSHIPS

For those still considering hotel investments, thorough market research is essential to identify locations with high tourist or business traveler demand. Partnering with experienced operators can help ensure operational excellence and high occupancy rates. However, even with experienced management, the investor's oversight and involvement are often required to maintain standards and profitability.

OUR RECOMMENDATION: CAUTION AND CLARITY OF GOALS

Given the intensive nature of hotel operations and the significant overhead costs, we recommend caution for investors seeking time freedom and lower operational involvement. If your time is tied up in this kind of business, you may not have the time to exponentially build your portfolio elsewhere. Hotels are not passive investments and require a hands-on approach, which may not align with the goals of investors like you who want time independence and lower overheads.

RV PARKS & GLAMPING:

GROWTH AND POTENTIAL

The outdoor hospitality sector, particularly RV parks and glamping, has witnessed remarkable growth. In 2020, the RV industry alone contributed over $114 billion to the U.S. economy. This surge is driven by a growing desire for outdoor experiences, eco-friendly travel options, and the flexibility to explore remote locations. RV parks and glamping sites offer a unique blend of nature and comfort, appealing to a broad demographic, from adventure-seeking millennials to retirees.

STRATEGIES FOR SUCCESS IN RV PARKS AND GLAMPING

1. Location Scouting: The Cornerstone of Success

- **Scenic and Accessible:** Ideal locations are those that blend scenic beauty with accessibility. Look for sites near natural attractions like national parks, beaches, or mountains. Proximity to major highways can also be beneficial for accessibility.

- **Local Attractions:** Consider areas that offer additional attractions or activities, like hiking trails, water sports, or cultural landmarks, adding value to the guest experience.

- **Climate Considerations:** Areas with favorable weather conditions for most of the year can ensure longer operating seasons and consistent revenue.

2. Experience Creation: Differentiating Your Offering

- **Unique Amenities:** Stand out by offering amenities like high-speed Wi-Fi, upscale bathhouses, boutique-style decor in glamping tents, or private hot tubs. These amenities cater to guests looking for comfort while embracing the outdoor experience.

- **Guided Tours and Activities:** Offering or partnering with local businesses to provide guided tours, outdoor activities, or workshops can significantly enhance the guest experience. Activities like guided hikes, fishing excursions, or local craft workshops add a unique dimension to the stay.

- **Community Building:** Create communal spaces like fire pits, communal kitchens, or event areas where guests can socialize. Hosting events like outdoor movie nights, stargazing sessions, or local food tastings can foster a sense of community.

3. Marketing and Branding: Reaching Your Audience

- **Digital Presence:** A strong online presence is crucial. Invest in a professional website, active social media engagement, and partnerships with online booking platforms.

- **Targeted Marketing:** Understand your target demographic and tailor your marketing efforts accordingly. Utilize digital marketing tools like SEO, content marketing, and social media advertising to reach potential guests.

- **Customer Reviews and Feedback:** Encourage and showcase customer reviews. Positive reviews on platforms like TripAdvisor or Google can significantly influence booking decisions.

4. Sustainability and Eco-Friendliness

- **Eco-Friendly Practices:** Implementing sustainable practices like solar power, composting toilets, and eco-friendly amenities can attract environmentally conscious guests and reduce operational costs.

- **Promotion of Local Ecology:** Educate guests about the local environment and promote conservation efforts. This approach not only enhances the guest experience but also helps in preserving the natural surroundings.

MOBILE HOME PARKS: COMPLICATED CASH COWS

Mobile Home Parks can be lucrative investments primarily due to their high cash flow potential. These properties often have lower acquisition and maintenance costs compared to traditional residential real estate, allowing for higher profit margins. The demand for affordable housing solutions, like those provided by mobile home parks, also contributes to their appeal as an investment.

UNDERSTANDING THE COMPLEXITIES

- **Cash Flow vs. Appreciation:** While mobile home parks can generate significant cash flow, they don't typically appreciate in value as much as other real estate assets. This is partly because the mobile home parks tend to negatively affect the value of real estate surrounding them.

- **Impact on Surrounding Real Estate:** Mobile home parks can sometimes negatively affect the value of surrounding properties. This perception issue can be due to various factors, including the density of the homes and the often transient nature of the residents.

- **Management Challenges:** Operating a mobile home park can be more management-intensive than other types of real estate. The success of these parks often hinges on effective and hands-on management, dealing with a range of tenant issues, maintenance, and sometimes the refurbishment of individual units.

LEGAL AND REGULATORY CONSIDERATIONS

- **Compliance with Regulations:** Stay informed about zoning laws, rent control regulations, and other legal requirements specific to mobile home parks in your area.

- **Infrastructure Investments:** Consider investing in the park's infrastructure, such as roads, utilities, and communal facilities, to maintain the property's value and appeal.

REITS:

While Real Estate Investment Trusts (REITs) offer an easy entry into real estate markets and are an excellent addition to retirement portfolios like 401(k)s or IRAs, they lack certain key advantages of direct real estate investment. One significant missing element is the ability to leverage investment capital.

- **Lack of Leverage:** Unlike direct property investments, where leverage (using borrowed capital for investment) can amplify returns and tax benefits, REITs typically don't offer this advantage. Investors in REITs miss out on the potential to control a large asset with a relatively small amount of personal capital.

- **Benefits in Retirement Portfolios:** Despite this limitation, REITs can play a vital role in a diversified retirement portfolio. Following models like the Swenson Model, REITs provide exposure to real estate markets without the complexity of managing properties, making them suitable for long-term, growth-oriented retirement accounts.

- **Tax Considerations:** REITs also offer tax advantages in retirement accounts, as their dividends are taxed as regular income. When held in tax-advantaged accounts like 401(k)s or IRAs, these dividends accumulate tax-free, adding to their appeal as a retirement investment.

HOW TO GET INVOLVED

- **Diversification Strategy:** While investing in REITs, diversify across various sectors like residential, commercial, healthcare, and industrial to balance risk.

- **Performance Monitoring:** Regularly evaluate the REITs in your portfolio for dividend yield, asset growth, and overall financial health.

TAX LIENS:

THE BASICS OF TAX LIEN INVESTING

Tax lien investing involves buying liens placed on properties due to unpaid taxes. When you purchase a tax lien, you essentially pay the tax debt of the property owner and in return, receive the right to collect the debt with interest. This investment can be lucrative, with interest rates ranging from 5% to 36%, depending on state laws.

HOW TO GET STARTED

- **Legal Know-How:** Each state has its own rules and periods for tax lien redemption. It's crucial to understand these legalities, including the process of foreclosure if the lien is not redeemed.

Risk Assessment: Conduct due diligence on each property before purchasing its tax lien. Evaluate factors like property value, location, and the likelihood of redemption. Some properties might seem like a bargain, but poor locations or conditions could make them difficult to sell if foreclosure is necessary.

- **Auction Participation:** Tax lien certificates are typically sold at auctions. Familiarize yourself with the auction process in the jurisdictions you are interested in and be prepared for competitive bidding.

PRIVATE LENDING:

HARD MONEY PRIVATE LENDING: AN OVERVIEW

Hard Money Private Lending is a form of short-term lending primarily used by real estate investors to finance property acquisitions and renovations. As a private lender in this market, you provide loans secured by real estate, with terms typically ranging from a few months to a few years. This approach is particularly appealing due to its potential for high returns and quick capital turnover.

ADVANTAGES OF HARD MONEY LENDING

- **Higher Interest Rates and Fees:** You can charge 1 or 2 points upfront (each point equals 1% of the loan amount) and then an annualized interest rate of 10-12% on the loan balance. These rates are typically higher than traditional bank loans.

- **Faster Capital Turnover:** By lending to fix-and-flip investors or builders, your capital can be deployed and returned quickly, often within a year. This rapid turnover allows you to reinvest your capital multiple times per year, compounding your investment.

GETTING INVOLVED IN HARD MONEY LENDING

- **Building a Network:** Connect with real estate investors, especially those involved in flipping houses or developing properties. Networking is key to finding reputable borrowers. Attend real estate investment meetings, participate in online forums, and engage with local real estate communities.

- **Due Diligence:** Assess the borrower's track record, creditworthiness, and the project's viability. Evaluate the property's value and the potential return on investment. Ensure that the loan-to-value (LTV) ratio is within a safe range to protect your investment.

- **Legal Framework:** Work with legal professionals to create sound lending agreements. This should include clear terms on points, interest rates, repayment schedules, and the process in case of default. Proper documentation is crucial to safeguard your investment.

PART 3: EFFICIENCY AT-SCALE

SIX

MAXIMIZING WEALTH WITH MULTIFAMILY INVESTMENTS

Walking into a free seminar in a hotel lobby, I had no inkling that I was stepping into a moment that would pivot my life altogether. They say big doors swing on small hinges, and that day, the truth of this saying couldn't have been more evident.

As I scanned the room, feeling somewhat out of place, I locked eyes with a familiar face from my men's mental health nonprofit - Fire Nights. The coincidence of meeting an old friend in that sea of aspiring investors felt like a nudge from fate. We were both there, in that room, hungry to learn about the world of multifamily investing—a concept that, until then, seemed leagues beyond my reach.

The idea of entering the multifamily market felt daunting, almost laughable, with my bank account not even close to ready for a $10 million investment. Yet, as the seminar unfolded, a door to a world I thought was locked tight began to crack open. The concept of syndication, pooling resources and expertise to invest in properties, transformed my view of what was possible. It was a revelation; we didn't need to have deep pockets to start. We just needed the right strategy and the willingness to take a leap.

Buoyed by this newfound knowledge and a serendipitous meeting, my friend Mike and I decided to dive in. Within three months of that seminar, we formed a partnership together that would lay the foundation for what would become Impact Investment Partners. Our first venture together was for $4.5MM — a 90-door apartment complex in Texas in need of significant rehabilitation. Thirty of those ninety units were severely damaged by water, presenting us with an incredible challenge but also an incredible opportunity to quickly pump in equity. Within a year that same property would already be worth over $10MM.

Mike brought with him an invaluable wealth of experience as the former CEO of Mercedes-Benz Club of America. His leadership skills and ability to connect with accredited investors and high-net-worth individuals propelled us into a realm of real estate investment I had once thought unattainable. Together, we embarked on a journey that would eventually become the most lucrative part of my entire real estate portfolio.

This chapter is your blueprint for anyone feeling sidelined in the game of multifamily investing, thinking the barrier to entry is too high. Here, I'll share how with the right knowledge, connections, and a bit of creativity, even the most daunting investments can be within your grasp. Let's explore how you, too, can unlock the door to multifamily investing, step through it, and change the course of your financial future, just as Mike and I did with Impact Investment Partners.

THE POWER OF MULTIFAMILY

Multifamily properties stand out as a powerhouse in real estate investing, distinguished by their exceptional capacity for wealth generation and risk mitigation. These properties, encompassing apartment buildings and other multi-unit residences, present investors with a unique array of advantages that outshine many traditional real estate investment strategies. Their prominence and dependability stem from a distinct blend of features that position them as a more secure and potentially more profitable choice than many other investment types, including the often fluctuating stock market.

The comparative safety of multifamily real estate investments is a well-established reality, not merely a perception. Reflecting on the past 15 years, we've seen the stock market undergo significant turbulence, exemplified by the 2008 financial crisis. This period starkly illustrated the volatility inherent in stock market investments, with many investors suffering substantial losses. In contrast, multifamily real estate has consistently demonstrated its resilience and stability. This asset class thrives on the ever-present need for housing, guaranteeing a steady cash flow. Furthermore, the typical appreciation in value of multifamily properties provides a buffer against the underperformance common in other investment domains.

The revenue model of multifamily properties solidifies their role as a wise investment choice. Contrasting with single-family residences, which depend on a singular income stream, multifamily properties benefit from housing multiple tenants. This diversity in revenue sources significantly diminishes financial risk. Should a tenant vacate, the effect on the property's overall cash flow is cushioned by the remaining occupants, ensuring that financial commitments, such as mortgage and maintenance expenses, continue to be met.

Recent shifts in living preferences further enhance the allure of multifamily investments. More and more renters, including a significant number of Millennials, are choosing multifamily arrangements. This enduring trend underlines a robust demand for such properties, securing their investment stability and potential for growth.

The financing of multifamily properties is typically more accommodating to investors compared to single-family units. Lenders often prioritize the income-generating capacity of the property over the personal financial circumstances of the investor. This approach minimizes financial risk for passive investors and frequently obviates the need for personal loan guarantees, an especially beneficial aspect.

Investors wield considerable influence over the performance of their multifamily properties, a facet that greatly enhances their investment appeal. Unlike investments in stocks or startups, where external factors like market fluctuations or company management decisions play a significant role, multifamily property investors can directly impact their investment's profitability. This control can manifest in various forms, from optimizing operational costs and adjusting rental rates to undertaking strategic property enhancements.

Operational efficiency is another key attribute of multifamily properties. Managing a single property with multiple units is often more cost-efficient on a per-unit basis than overseeing an equivalent number of single-family homes. This efficiency leads to increased net operating income (NOI), a vital determinant of the property's value.

The correlation between NOI and property valuation is a crucial aspect of multifamily investing. A rise in NOI, achieved through strategies like rent optimization or cost reduction, can significantly enhance a property's worth. For instance, a $1 million increase in NOI can, assuming a 5% cap rate, elevate the property's value by $20 million, illustrating the potential for substantial value appreciation.

In addition to the benefits of consistent cash flow and economies of scale, multifamily properties represent not just a secure investment but a powerful one. The capability to manage and strategically upgrade these properties can lead to significant wealth accumulation, positioning multifamily real estate investing as one of the most effective means of building and sustaining wealth in the real estate sector.

Finally, and importantly, the tax advantages associated with real estate investments, particularly multifamily properties, are unparalleled. Investors have the opportunity to reduce their taxable income significantly through deductions for various expenses. The unique benefit of depreciation in real estate allows for accounting for the property's wear and tear over time, further diminishing taxable income. This aspect of tax strategy is where multifamily properties truly shine above other asset classes, playing a pivotal role in the accumulation of wealth.

If that sounds appealing to you, I'm going to walk you through in the rest of this chapter exactly how to dive into and succeed in Multifamily investing. It's hard work and a challenging learning curve, but don't close the book if it seems overwhelming. In the next chapter I'll show you how to do the same thing, but much, much more simple. I call it the Easy Button.

THE ACQUISITION PROCESS

Acquiring multifamily properties may seem complex at first, but over time it will become second nature to you as you multiply your assets and cashflow. The first step is simply identifying an emerging market. This initial stage involves general research to pinpoint areas with a growing population and an increasing demand for housing, thus ensuring a robust investment potential. Once a suitable market is found, the focus shifts to identifying properties that align with your investment criteria, taking into account factors such as location, condition, and potential for rental growth. The best approach to finding a deal will be finding off-market properties. I'll give you strategies for this later in the chapter.

When you have selected a potential property, it will be time to talk with the broker and draft a Letter of Intent (LOI). The LOI signifies your interest in acquiring the property and outlines the preliminary terms of the purchase. While not legally binding, the LOI serves as a formal gesture to initiate negotiations and demonstrates your seriousness as a buyer.

Upon agreeing on preliminary terms and having the LOI in place, a thorough financial analysis is conducted. This involves delving into the property's financial statements, assessing key metrics like cap rate, cash-on-cash return, and internal rate of return (IRR). Future cash flow projections are also crucial at this stage, taking into account potential changes in rent, occupancy rates, and operational efficiencies.

The due diligence phase is where the acquisition process becomes particularly hands-on. During this phase, it's common to physically visit the property, especially if it's located out of state. This visit is not just a cursory walkthrough; it's an opportunity to conduct a detailed inspection and to meet with various professionals on-site. You'll consult with engineers, contractors, plumbers, and electricians to get estimates on all planned value-add improvements. This on-the-ground assessment is vital for a comprehensive understanding of the property's condition and the scope of any necessary renovations. Importantly, the expenses incurred during this trip are often reimbursed at closing, making it a worthwhile investment.

If any issues or potential value-add opportunities are uncovered during due diligence, you may engage in retrading. Retrading involves renegotiating the terms of the deal, particularly the price, to account for new information that impacts the property's value. It's a critical component of the process that ensures the investment is aligned with its true worth.

Following successful due diligence and any retrading, the final terms of the deal are encapsulated in the Purchase and Sale Agreement (PSA). This legally binding document outlines all the agreed-upon terms of the transaction, including price, contingencies, and closing conditions. The PSA is a pivotal component of the acquisition process, solidifying the agreement between buyer and seller.

With the PSA in hand, securing financing becomes the next crucial step. This involves negotiating with lenders to obtain favorable mortgage terms that reflect the property's income potential, taking into account any adjustments made during retrading.

The acquisition process culminates in the closing, where all legal and financial formalities are completed, and ownership of the property is officially transferred.

Post-acquisition, your focus will shift to implementing the operational and management strategies planned during the due diligence phase, including undertaking any value-add renovations and improvements identified.

BUILDING YOUR TEAM

Success in any venture requires you to dive in and learn as you go, but don't forget that multifamily properties are highly complicated investments that inherently hold risk. So don't try to figure it all out by yourself. You will have blind spots. Find people with experience who can do the hard work for you and can show you the ropes along the way.

GENERAL PARTNERS

1. **Acquisitions Specialist/Underwriter**: This is the person who identifies, analyzes, and secures potential investment opportunities. They need a keen eye for profitable properties and a deep understanding of market dynamics.

2. **Asset Manager**: Responsible for the operational and financial performance of the property. They work to maximize revenue and control expenses.

3. **Sponsor**: Typically, a sponsor brings financial credibility and experience to the deal, often signing loan guarantees and bringing a successful track record.

KEY PARTNERS IN YOUR TARGET MARKET

1. **Commercial/Multifamily Brokers**: These professionals are your gateway to off-market deals and insider market knowledge.

2. **SEC Attorney**: Essential for ensuring compliance with securities laws, especially if you're raising capital from investors.

3. **Title Attorney**: They play a crucial role in navigating the complexities of property titles and closing the deal.

Property Management Companies: Managing a multifamily property is a significant task. Partnering with skilled property managers is crucial for maintaining the property and tenant relations.

5. **Commercial Construction Company**: Usually the property management company or your asset manager will have a construction company that they have a good working relationship with. However in some cases it will be your responisbility to find a good local one when evaluating properties.

6. **Architect / Design Firm:** Often times here your sponsor will have recommendations if you don't know where to start. I have a dear friend who has a great Design Firm so I use him for all of our projects. You will want to begin to build a relationship with one local to where you live so you can deeply collaborate with the design team when dealing with big value-add projects, new builds, and re-branding for your apartment complex. You can continue to work with this design team with all future investments as well.

7. **Real Estate CPA**: Specialized in real estate, they can guide you through the nuances of real estate taxation. The CPA will also help generate your reports for your investors.

8. **Coach/Mentor**: Someone with multifamily experience can offer invaluable advice and help you avoid common pitfalls. Reach out to us if you're looking for a guide into this new investment space.

UNDERWRITING: KNOW YOUR NUMBERS

Multifamily investing is a numbers game, and understanding these key financial metrics is non-negotiable. Let's break down the essential numbers that drive multifamily investments:

1. CAP RATE (CAPITALIZATION RATE)

Cap rate is the foundational metric in real estate. It's the annual rate of return you would receive if you bought a property with cash. In multifamily investing, cap rates vary by market and property class. Understanding cap rates helps you assess risk and potential returns.

2. DSCR (DEBT SERVICE COVERAGE RATIO)

DSCR measures your property's ability to cover its debt obligations. It's calculated by dividing your property's net operating income (NOI) by its debt service (mortgage payments). Lenders typically look for a DSCR of 1.25 or higher, ensuring that your property generates enough income to cover debt.

3. CASH ON CASH RETURN

Cash on cash return gauges the annual return on your invested capital. It considers the cash flow generated by the property in relation to your initial investment, including down payment and closing costs. A higher cash on cash return signifies better returns on your invested capital.

4. CASH FLOW

Cash flow is the lifeblood of multifamily investments. It's the money left over after paying all expenses, including mortgage, property management, maintenance, and taxes. Positive cash flow ensures your property remains a profitable venture.

5. CAPITAL RESERVES

Capital reserves are funds set aside for future property expenses and unexpected repairs. Maintaining adequate reserves is crucial to safeguard your investment against unforeseen events.

6. ACQUISITION FEE

The acquisition fee is a one-time payment made to your sponsor or acquisitions specialist for securing the deal. It's typically a percentage of the purchase price. Understanding this fee structure is essential to budgeting for your investment.

7. INSURANCE

Insurance protects your investment from unforeseen events such as natural disasters or accidents. It's a critical component of risk management in multifamily investing.

8. NOI (NET OPERATING INCOME)

Net Operating Income is the total income generated by your property after subtracting operating expenses. It's a key metric used to assess the property's profitability.

These financial metrics provide the foundation for analyzing potential multifamily deals. Mastery of these numbers is vital to making informed investment decisions and ensuring the financial success of your properties.

9**. 65% - 75% FANNIE AND FREDDIE**

Fannie Mae and Freddie Mac are government-sponsored entities that offer competitive loan programs for multifamily properties. These agencies provide financing options with favorable terms, making them popular choices among investors.

10**. 25%-30% DOWN PAYMENT**

To secure financing, you'll typically need to make a down payment ranging from 25% to 30% of the property's purchase price. This equity injection demonstrates your commitment to the investment and mitigates risk for lenders.

11**. CAPITAL EXPENDITURES**

Capital expenditures (CapEx) cover significant property improvements and renovations. Setting aside funds for CapEx is crucial for maintaining and enhancing the property's value over time.

12**. CLOSING COSTS**

Closing costs include fees associated with finalizing the real estate transaction. These expenses can vary but typically include attorney fees, title insurance, acquisition fees, and appraisal costs.

FINDING A DEAL

Securing a multifamily property is the heart of your investment journey. Knowing where to find deals and how to evaluate them is paramount. Let's explore the avenues to uncover promising multifamily opportunities:

1. EMERGING MARKET

Emerging markets offer immense potential for multifamily investors. These are areas experiencing population growth, job creation, and economic expansion. Investing in an emerging market can lead to higher demand for apartments and potential for property appreciation.

2. OFF-MARKET PROPERTIES

Off-market properties are gems hidden from the public eye. They often represent unique opportunities with less competition. Building relationships with local brokers and networking in the industry can lead you to these off-market treasures.

3. POCKET LISTINGS

Pocket listings are exclusive offerings by brokers to a select group of investors. These listings are not widely advertised, giving you an advantage in negotiations. Cultivating strong relationships with brokers can grant you access to these off-market gems.

4. ONLINE COMMERCIAL PLATFORMS

The digital age has transformed real estate searching. Online platforms like LoopNet.com, Crexi.com, CoStar.com, and Realtor.com have extensive listings. Utilize these platforms to explore properties, assess market trends, and identify potential investments.

Finding the right deal is often a blend of diligence, networking, and market knowledge. As you build your multifamily investing career, you'll refine your deal-finding strategies, uncovering opportunities that others might overlook.

6. ASSET MANAGEMENT

Once you've acquired a multifamily property, effective asset management is key to maximizing its potential. Asset management essentially manages the property manager and responds to emergencies on behalf of the team. Asset managers oversee day-to-day operations, including tenant relations, property maintenance, and financial management. They ensure that the property is running smoothly and profitably.

2. EQUITY PARTNER + CASH FLOW

As an equity partner, you are responsible for the long-term vision of the property. Your focus is on wealth creation through property appreciation and equity buildup. Key responsibilities include:

- **Value-Add Strategies**: Implement value-add strategies to increase the property's value over time. This might involve renovations, improving amenities, or optimizing rents.

Property Upkeep: Ensure the property is well-maintained. A well-kept property attracts quality tenants and retains its value.

- **Market Monitoring**: Stay attuned to market trends and adjust your strategies accordingly. Being proactive in response to changing market conditions is vital.

While building equity is a long-term play, you also benefit from the immediate income generated by the property. This cash flow can be a valuable source of passive income. Your responsibilities as a cash flow recipient include:

- **Financial Oversight**: Review monthly financial statements to ensure that the property is meeting its income and expense projections.

- **Budgeting**: Work with your property management team to set and monitor budgets. Effective budgeting helps maintain positive cash flow.

- **Tenant Relations**: Though day-to-day tenant interactions are managed by your property management team, being aware of tenant concerns and addressing them promptly can help maintain a healthy income stream.

Balancing these dual roles requires effective communication with your property management team and a keen eye on your investment goals. Your ability to grow your wealth while enjoying consistent cash flow is a testament to the multifaceted benefits of multifamily investing.

EXIT STRATEGY

Start with the end in mind. Your exit strategy is more than just a plan for when you decide to sell your multifamily property; it's your business plan. It defines your investment goals, risk tolerance, and desired outcomes. As an investor, understanding your exit strategy is like having a compass that guides your decisions throughout the investment lifecycle.

THE CATALYST FOR PROFIT

Though you can invest in turn-key multifamily assets, you lack the ability to inject value into the property through Capital Expenditures. That's why the most powerful approach to multifamily investing utilizes value-add strategies. These are proactive steps taken to increase a property's value, enhance its income-generating potential, and position it for a profitable exit. Value-add initiatives can encompass a wide range of improvements, including:

- **Renovations**: Upgrading unit interiors, common areas, and amenities to attract higher-paying tenants.

-

Expense Reduction: Identifying cost-saving measures to improve the property's overall financial performance.

- **Revenue Optimization**: Increasing rental income through strategic rent increases, lease renewals, or ancillary income sources.

- **Property Repositioning**: Repositioning the property within its market segment to cater to a different tenant demographic.

Value-add strategies are integral to your exit plan because they directly impact the property's market value. By enhancing the property's financial performance and desirability, you're setting the stage for a more lucrative exit.

SELL IN 3-5 YEARS: VELOCITY OF MONEY AND OPPORTUNITY COST

One common exit strategy for multifamily investors is to sell the property within 3-5 years of acquisition. This approach offers several advantages:

VELOCITY OF MONEY

Selling in a relatively short time frame allows you to recycle your capital more quickly. When you sell a property and realize a profit, you can reinvest that capital into new opportunities. This concept, known as the velocity of money, is a powerful wealth-building tool. It enables you to leverage your initial investment across multiple properties and increase your overall returns.

MINIMIZING OPPORTUNITY COST

Opportunity cost refers to the potential gains you forgo by choosing one investment over another. By selling within 3-5 years, you reduce the opportunity cost associated with tying up your capital in a single property for an extended period. This approach allows you to explore other multifamily opportunities that may offer better returns or align with your evolving investment goals.

SELL IN 5-10 YEARS: BUY AND HOLD FOR CASH FLOW

Another viable exit strategy is to hold onto the multifamily property for a more extended period, typically between 5 and 10 years. This approach is characterized by a focus on cash flow and long-term wealth building. Here's why it might be the right choice for some investors:

CASH FLOW EMPHASIS

Buying and holding for an extended period prioritizes consistent cash flow as the primary source of return on investment. It's an approach suited for investors who value a steady stream of passive income and are less concerned with rapid capital appreciation.

WEALTH BUILDING

Over time, rental income from a well-managed multifamily property can contribute significantly to your wealth. As the property appreciates, the equity you build becomes a valuable asset that can be leveraged for future investments or used as a source of retirement income.

CAP RATE: THE RISK INDICATOR

Regardless of your chosen exit strategy, it's crucial to keep a close eye on the property's capitalization rate, or cap rate. The cap rate represents the risk associated with your investment. Understanding its significance is vital for making informed exit decisions.

HIGH CASH FLOW AND CAP RATE

Properties with high cash flow often have a correspondingly high cap rate. While this may seem attractive for immediate returns, it can signal higher perceived risk in the market. Such properties are typically located in markets with lower barriers to entry, which can lead to increased competition and, potentially, lower long-term appreciation.

EMERGING MARKETS AND EQUITY BUILDING

In contrast, successful investors often base their business models on emerging markets rather than solely on cash flow. These emerging markets may have lower initial cap rates but offer the potential for substantial equity and wealth building over time. Investing with an eye on long-term appreciation and market growth can yield more significant returns in the end.

Investing in multifamily real estate is not a one-size-fits-all solution. It's a dynamic aspect of your investment plan that should align with your goals, risk tolerance, and market conditions. Whether you opt for a shorter-term exit to leverage the velocity of money or a more extended buy-and-hold approach for cash flow and wealth building, your exit strategy is a pivotal component of your multifamily journey.

As a multifamily investor, you possess the flexibility to adapt your exit strategy as circumstances evolve. The key is to remain vigilant, monitor market trends, and adjust your plan to maximize returns and achieve your financial objectives. Ultimately, your exit strategy is the compass that guides you toward your destination—a successful and prosperous multifamily investment portfolio.

Now in this next chapter I am going to teach you the easiest way to transform your portfolio with Multifamily investing where you don't even have to do any of the acquisition nor management of the asset.

SEVEN

THE EASY BUTTON - PASSIVE MULTIFAMILY INVESTMENT

My friend from Salt Lake City, with a rich background in residential real estate, wanted to scale the heights of apartment investing. However, he faced a steep learning curve in this new domain. His solution? To start as a Limited Partner (LP) and utilize it as his "Easy Ramp" into the multifamily sector.

What made this route particularly appealing was the unique structure of the LP-GP relationship in multifamily investments. The General Partners (GPs) take on the heavy lifting—finding deals, analyzing potential returns, qualifying for loans, selecting and managing the property management company. Essentially, the GPs are the architects and the builders, ensuring the investment's success from groundwork to peak.

For my friend, being an LP meant he could learn the ropes without getting tangled in them. While the GP team handled the intricacies of the deals, he had the luxury of sitting back, absorbing the process, and receiving quarterly updates on the investment's performance. More than just updates, these quarters often came with dividends, making his learning journey not just informative but also financially rewarding.

This model of investing allowed him to observe the strategies and decisions of experienced GPs up close. Every aspect of the deal, from the initial analysis to the ongoing management of the property, was a lesson in multifamily investing, served on a silver platter. He was learning from the best, seeing firsthand how to navigate the challenges and opportunities of multifamily investments without the immediate pressure of being in charge.

Transitioning from a passive observer to an active leader, my friend's path from LP to GP was marked by significant growth and success. Now managing over $250 million in assets, his story is a powerful testament to the "Easy Ramp" approach. It highlights the value of starting as an LP, where you can gain critical insights and build a solid foundation in multifamily investing while the GPs manage the day-to-day complexities.

For anyone looking to break into multifamily investments, remember: there's a way to learn the trade without being overwhelmed by its demands. By starting as an LP, you can enjoy the dual benefits of educational growth and financial returns, all while the GPs handle the operational challenges.

Transitioning from a passive observer to an active leader, my friend's path from LP to GP was marked by significant growth and success, managing over $250 million in assets. However, it's important to note that his story might differ from yours. You might not be aiming to become a General Partner, and that's perfectly okay. The beauty of passive investing as a Limited Partner is that it's a strategy employed by many savvy investors, including billionaires, to keep their wealth actively growing without the need for direct involvement in the day-to-day operations.

As a Limited Partner, your role is pretty straightforward: you bring the cash. You leave the heavy lifting to the General Partners. For those who prefer focusing on their passions or other ventures, being an LP offers a way to participate in the dig deals without the complexities of management and operations. It allows you to leverage the expertise of seasoned GPs who handle everything from deal acquisition to property management. In this way, your money is not just sitting idle; it's working for you, generating quarterly updates and often dividends, allowing you to enjoy the financial rewards of real estate investment without diverting time and energy away from your main interests.

This approach to investing underscores a broader principle in wealth management: the power of passive income streams in building and preserving wealth. By choosing to be an LP in multifamily deals, you're adopting a strategy that enables your capital to grow, benefiting from the expertise of others while you concentrate on what you love. Whether or not you decide to take a more active role in real estate investments down the line, starting as an LP can provide a solid foundation, financial returns, and perhaps most importantly, the freedom to pursue your passions.

Limited Partners vs. General Partners

When diving into multifamily investments, it's crucial to understand the distinct roles and benefits of Limited Partners (LPs) and General Partners (GPs), especially in terms of responsibilities and tax advantages.

General Partners: Carrying the Weight of the Investment

General Partners act as the cornerstone of any multifamily real estate investment. They're the strategists and the day-to-day managers, shouldering the bulk of the workload. This 'heavy lifting' includes:

- **Operational Management:** GPs handle all aspects of property management, from tenant relations to maintenance and renovations.

- **Strategic Decision-Making:** They make key decisions, like when to buy or sell properties, optimizing for market conditions.

- **Financial Oversight:** GPs manage the property's finances, including budgeting, rent collection, and expense management.

- **Legal and Compliance Responsibilities:** They ensure that the investment complies with all relevant laws and regulations.

In return for their extensive involvement and higher risk, GPs often receive a larger share of the profits once the LPs have received their agreed-upon returns.

EMBRACING THE PASSIVE INVESTMENT MODEL

The passive nature of investing as a Limited Partner (LP) in multifamily real estate is one of its most appealing aspects, particularly for those looking to diversify their investment portfolio without taking on the time-consuming responsibilities of the General Partners.

At its core, passive investing as an LP allows individuals to invest in real estate without being involved in the day-to-day operations of property management. This means investors can reap the benefits of real estate ownership—such as income generation, property appreciation, and tax advantages—without the burdens that come with being a landlord or property manager.

KEY FEATURES OF PASSIVE INVESTING

- **Hands-off Approach:** As an LP, your primary responsibility is to provide capital for the investment. The General Partners (GPs) take care of finding deals, conducting due diligence, securing financing, managing renovations, and handling tenant relations. This setup is ideal for investors who prefer to focus on their careers, businesses, or other interests.

- **Quarterly Updates and Dividends:** Despite the passive role, LPs stay informed through regular updates from the GP team, often including financial statements and project progress reports. Many investments distribute quarterly dividends, providing a tangible return on investment that complements the passive nature of the stake.

- **Risk Mitigation:** The limited liability status of LPs protects personal assets beyond the invested capital. This protection is crucial for investors looking to mitigate risk while enjoying the potential upside of real estate investments.

BALANCING PASSIVE INVESTING WITH ACTIVE OVERSIGHT

While the investment is passive, savvy LPs engage in periodic due diligence to ensure their investment continues to align with their goals. This might include reviewing quarterly reports, staying updated on market trends affecting the property's performance, and maintaining open communication with GPs. Such active oversight ensures that the investment remains on track without requiring day-to-day involvement.

THE IDEAL CANDIDATE FOR PASSIVE INVESTING

Passive investing in multifamily assets is especially suited for individuals who:

- Seek to diversify their investment portfolio into real estate without adding to their daily workload.

- Have capital to invest but prefer to avoid the complexities and time commitment of property management.

-

Wish to leverage the expertise of experienced real estate professionals to potentially increase their returns.

- Value the protection of personal assets and appreciate the structure of limited liability.

Tax Heaven

Investing passively in multifamily real estate offers definitive tax benefits that enhance wealth accumulation and optimize tax efficiency. These advantages stem from the unique characteristics of real estate investments and the specific provisions in the tax code designed to encourage property investment and development. Here's a detailed examination of the key tax benefits that directly impact LPs:

DEPRECIATION

Depreciation is a tax deduction that reflects the cost of the property's physical deterioration over time. For commercial real estate, this period is set at 39 years by the IRS.

- **Impact:** Depreciation significantly reduces the taxable income generated by the property, lowering the overall tax liability for the investment. LPs benefit proportionally to their investment stake, utilizing depreciation to offset income and reduce taxes owed.

MORTGAGE INTEREST DEDUCTION

Interest on loans taken out for purchasing or improving the property is fully deductible against the property's income. This encompasses mortgage and construction loans.

- **Impact:** This deduction lowers the net taxable income of the property, effectively reducing the income tax due by the partnership and, by extension, the individual LPs.

PASS-THROUGH DEDUCTIONS

The Tax Cuts and Jobs Act enables a deduction of up to 20% of business income for certain pass-through entities, including partnerships and LLCs typically used for real estate investments.

- **Impact:** Eligible LPs receive a deduction of up to 20% of their share of the entity's income, substantially lowering their taxable income. It is crucial for LPs to consult with tax professionals to navigate the specific requirements and limitations.

1031 EXCHANGE OPPORTUNITIES

A 1031 exchange allows the deferral of capital gains taxes on the sale of a property when the proceeds are reinvested in a similar property.

- **Impact:** LPs directly benefit from their share in a 1031 exchange, allowing the reinvestment of proceeds into new real estate investments without incurring immediate capital gains taxes. This provision facilitates the compounding of investment gains over time without the reduction of capital gains taxes.

- Note: For our funds through Impact Investment Partners, we do not allow 1031 Exchanges unless they are bringing more than $1,000,000 to the table on a deal because of the added complexity. That is the common practice for syndication models.

TAX-FREE CASH FLOW VIA REFINANCING

Refinancing a property that has increased in value can provide cash distributions that are not considered taxable income but rather a return of capital.

- **Impact:** LPs enjoy distributions without immediate tax implications, improving the investment's cash-on-cash return and deferring taxes until the property's eventual sale.

THE MAGIC OF BONUS DEPRECIATION

Navigating the complexities of multifamily real estate investments is greatly facilitated by the insights and expertise of a seasoned General Partner (GP) team, especially when it comes to leveraging tax incentives like 100% Bonus Depreciation. This section offers a practical example that highlights the critical role of experienced GPs in utilizing Bonus Depreciation to enhance the financial outcomes of such investments.

SCENARIO: STRATEGIC ENHANCEMENT AND TAX PLANNING

Consider Jordan, a Limited Partner (LP), who invests in a multifamily property managed by an adept GP team. In the inaugural year of their venture, they collectively decide to undertake significant improvements—specifically, upgrading the HVAC system, installing a new roofing solution, and overhauling the security system, with a cumulative expenditure of $500,000. These targeted improvements qualify for 100% Bonus Depreciation, a fact astutely identified by the GP team for its strategic tax advantages.

THE PIVOTAL ROLE OF EXPERIENCED GPS

The GP team, with their profound understanding of real estate investment dynamics and tax legislation, identifies this opportunity to not only elevate the property's market value and tenant appeal but also to employ a strategic tax planning measure. They recognize that under prevailing tax laws, the partnership can fully deduct the $500,000 investment in the year these improvements are completed, thanks to the provision of 100% Bonus Depreciation.

FINANCIAL AND TAX IMPLICATIONS

Against a backdrop of $300,000 in rental income for the year, the immediate deduction of the $500,000 in improvement costs substantially lowers the taxable income of the partnership. This move diverges from the standard practice of depreciating such improvements over a 27.5-year lifespan, which would typically yield a modest annual depreciation expense of around $18,182.

Before Bonus Depreciation: Utilizing traditional depreciation methods would leave a considerable portion of the rental income exposed to taxation.

- **With 100% Bonus Depreciation:** The partnership can deduct the entire improvement cost in the first year, potentially reducing the taxable income to a negative value, thereby generating a $200,000 tax loss. This strategic loss can then be leveraged to offset other forms of income, markedly lowering the partnership's—and by extension, Jordan's—overall tax liability for the year.

LEVERAGING GP EXPERTISE

The example underscores the invaluable role played by the GP team in managing property operations, spearheading improvement initiatives, and strategically navigating tax incentives such as Bonus Depreciation to optimize investment returns. Their decisions are informed by a comprehensive understanding of tax laws and a commitment to achieving the best possible financial outcomes for their investors.

RISK MANAGEMENT IN PASSIVE MULTIFAMILY INVESTMENTS

For Limited Partners (LPs) investing in multifamily real estate, understanding and managing risk is paramount to safeguarding and growing their investments. While the passive nature of an LP's investment means less direct control over daily operations, there are strategic ways LPs can evaluate and mitigate risks associated with their investments. One of the most effective strategies is investing alongside a team of experienced General Partners (GPs).

EVALUATING AND MANAGING RISK AS AN LP

Diversification: One fundamental risk management strategy is diversification, not just across real estate assets, but also across markets and investment types. LPs can spread their investments across different properties and geographical locations to mitigate the impact of local market downturns.

Due Diligence: Before committing capital, LPs should conduct thorough due diligence on the property, the market, and most importantly, the GP team. Understanding the track record, expertise, and strategy of the GP can significantly reduce investment risk.

Legal Structure and Terms: LPs must be familiar with the legal structure of the investment and the specific terms of their involvement. This includes understanding their rights, obligations, and the conditions under which their capital is managed and returned. Clear exit strategies and distribution waterfalls should be established upfront.

Market and Economic Trends: Keeping informed about broader market and economic trends can help LPs anticipate changes that might affect their investments. While LPs are not involved in day-to-day management, having a macro perspective can aid in making informed decisions about starting, continuing, or exiting an investment.

MINIMIZING RISK WITH EXPERIENCED GPS

Expertise and Experience: A seasoned GP team brings invaluable market insights, operational expertise, and strategic foresight. Their experience in navigating various market cycles, managing properties efficiently, and optimizing financial structures can significantly mitigate investment risks.

Strategic Decision-Making: Experienced GPs make informed, strategic decisions about property acquisitions, financing, improvements, and when to sell or refinance. Their ability to make timely decisions based on comprehensive market analysis and property performance data can protect and enhance the value of the investment.

Operational Efficiency: GPs with a proven track record manage properties effectively, ensuring high occupancy rates, stable rental income, and controlled operating expenses. Their expertise in selecting and overseeing property management can directly impact the investment's success.

Risk Mitigation Strategies: Skilled GPs implement sophisticated risk mitigation strategies, including adequate insurance coverage, conservative financial structuring, and contingency planning for unexpected market shifts or economic downturns.

EXPLORING INVESTMENT VEHICLES: SYNDICATIONS OR FUND OF FUNDS

For passive investors aiming to diversify their portfolios through multifamily real estate, choosing the right investment vehicle is critical. Two prominent options are real estate syndications and funds of funds (FoFs), each offering distinct paths to investment success. Understanding the nuances of each can help investors make informed decisions that align with their investment goals, risk tolerance, and preference for involvement.

REAL ESTATE SYNDICATIONS: DIRECT INVESTMENT AND TRANSPARENCY

Real estate syndications involve a group of investors pooling their resources to purchase a property. This structure is managed by General Partners (GPs), who handle all aspects of the investment, from acquisition to management, while Limited Partners (LPs) contribute financially without taking part in the day-to-day operations.

Main Benefit: A significant advantage of investing in a syndication is the ability for LPs to thoroughly question and assess the assumptions of the deal due to its focus on a single property. This direct investment approach allows investors to:

- **Evaluate Detailed Assumptions:** LPs can examine specific financial models, projected returns, and risk factors with a level of detail not typically available in other investment vehicles.

- **Direct Communication with GPs:** This investment structure fosters transparent communication between LPs and GPs, enabling a clear understanding of the property's potential and strategic approach.

- **Focused Risk Assessment:** Investors can assess risks based on tangible factors affecting the property, including market dynamics, competitive positioning, and operational plans.

FUNDS OF FUNDS: DIVERSIFICATION AND COMPLEX EVALUATION

A fund of funds (FoF) invests in a portfolio of other funds, including multiple real estate syndications or other real estate investment vehicles, offering investors a diversified approach to real estate investment.

Considerations: While FoFs provide broad exposure to various markets and investment strategies, the assumptions underlying these investments are inherently more complex. This complexity is due to:

- **Diverse Investment Strategies:** FoFs encompass a range of properties, markets, and management teams, each with its own set of assumptions and market conditions.
- **Layered Management Approaches:** The combination of different funds introduces variability in investment outcomes, linked to the varied expertise and strategies of the underlying fund managers.
- **Subjective Risk and Return Evaluations:** Evaluating a FoF involves understanding the aggregated effect of multiple investment strategies, which can be more subjective and challenging for LPs to navigate directly.

The primary benefit of investing in a syndication for LPs is the ability to closely scrutinize the deal's assumptions, offering a level of transparency and direct evaluation that's more challenging to achieve in a fund of funds. Conversely, FoFs appeal to investors seeking diversified exposure across a range of real estate investments, albeit with a more complex and layered approach to understanding and assessing investment assumptions.

SIMPLY, THE BEST STRATEGY

Embarking on the path of passive investment in multifamily real estate is not just a journey towards financial growth; it's a leap towards achieving unparalleled wealth and stability. This chapter has illuminated the profound potential that lies within the realm of real estate, showcasing why it stands as the cornerstone of the portfolios of the affluent. It's the blend of lucrative returns, exceptional tax advantages, and strategic risk mitigation that sets multifamily real estate apart as the pinnacle of investment opportunities.

Multifamily real estate, through its inherent value and resilience, provides a unique vessel for wealth creation that is unmatched by any other asset class. The beauty of this investment strategy lies in its simplicity and effectiveness. By aligning with seasoned General Partners, passive investors gain access to a world where their capital works harder than ever before, not just earning income but also growing in value, all while benefiting from the extraordinary tax benefits exclusive to real estate.

This is why the most savvy and prosperous investors consistently turn to multifamily real estate. It's not merely an investment option;

it's a powerful tool for wealth accumulation, offering a balance of risk and return that is carefully calibrated for long-term success. The journey through multifamily real estate investing is one marked by strategic growth, learning, and the opportunity to contribute to something larger than oneself—a thriving community within a tangible asset that stands the test of time.

As you contemplate your next steps in the investment world, consider the unparalleled opportunities multifamily real estate presents. With the right team, the right strategy, and a keen understanding of the market, you can unlock a level of wealth and security that transcends the ordinary, propelling your portfolio to new heights. In the landscape of investment, multifamily real estate is not just a path but a gateway to achieving lasting financial freedom and legacy. There is, indeed, no other asset quite like it.

EIGHT

TAX SECRETS OF THE WEALTHY

What I want to do here for you feels like an impossible task. It's no small feat to unravel the mysteries of our 6,000 page Tax Code in a way that resonates with the everyday person. For most, taxes are a source of dread, a seemingly impenetrable labyrinth that leaves them feeling targeted by the intricacies of the tax law. Over the years, media and financial advisors have painted a grim picture, insisting that the tax code is a realm far too intricate for the average individual to grasp. However beneath the layers of complexity, the fundamentals of tax strategy are simple. The most wealthy people in this country use these fundamentals everyday, and after about a thousand hours of studying them and their approaches, I've found that what they do is simple. I will unpack all of this for you in this single chapter.

Here's where we'll start. Think of the carrot versus the stick: the tax code is about the carrot. Originally, tax laws were never designed with the common worker in mind; they were meant to tap into the excess earnings of the wealthiest individuals and corporations. But as time has passed, these laws have evolved into instruments of social and economic policy. The landscape of taxation has shifted, with employees bearing the heaviest tax burden while employers and investors enjoy lower rates. The reason? Economic policymakers finally began to understand that humans respond well to incentives.

If you want to foster larger families, offer a tax credit for each child. To encourage domestic oil production, provide significant tax deductions for investments in oil and gas. Building apartments for low-income workers? Reward investors with tax credits. The list goes on, illustrating how tax laws have transformed into tools of policy-making.

This chapter isn't a critique of our tax laws, nor can I fully unpack it in these pages. Taxes are an immutable part of our reality and will forever remain a fixture in our lives. Death and taxes, right? Instead of lamenting them, waiting for parliaments and legislatures to render them fairer, let's take a different route. Let's understand them and harness their power for our benefit. Let's chase that stick.

Taxes can be either the ticket to explosive growth or the anchor dragging us down. The tax laws of every nation are penned with a purpose – to encourage activities that invigorate the economy and serve social policy objectives. It is our responsibility to unravel these laws and make the most of them as they stand.

This chapter isn't about exploiting loopholes; it's about seizing the intended advantages. Loopholes are unforeseen consequences of enacted laws, whereas we focus on capitalizing on the outcomes that lawmakers intended. By investing where governments suggest, we garner tax benefits. By channeling our time and talents into endeavors that stimulate job growth, housing, and economic expansion, we earn tax rewards. In many ways, optimizing the tax code to minimize tax expenses is one of the most patriotic endeavors we can undertake.

While the specifics of tax law might appear daunting, this chapter won't turn you into an expert on your country's tax code. Instead, it will equip you with the core principles, empowering you to work within the system, as designed by your government. In doing so, you may discover that not only do your taxes decrease, but your profits and investment returns flourish. In essence, the tax law is a map – a treasure map. As you embark on this treasure hunt, your tax burden diminishes, and your financial freedom beckons tantalizingly close. So, let's embark on this journey and uncover the secrets of strategic tax planning that can open the door to financial prosperity.

A CASE STUDY: AMAZON

The story of Jeff Bezos and Amazon is a compelling narrative of starting small and dreaming big. In the early days, Bezos embarked on his ambitious journey from a modest garage, a space where dreams were nurtured and the seeds of an e-commerce revolution were planted. This wasn't just about selling books online; it was about reimagining the future of retail. Bezos' approach was rooted in learning as he went, embracing risks, and leveraging every failure as a stepping stone. His vision extended far beyond immediate profits, focusing instead on long-term growth, market expansion, and forward-thinking tax strategy.

Central to Amazon's strategy was a bold financial playbook: prioritize reinvestment over short-term earnings. This meant plowing revenues back into the company to build a formidable infrastructure, expand into untapped markets, and develop groundbreaking services like Amazon Web Services (AWS). Such a vision demanded not just patience but also a strategic engagement with the financial intricacies of running a burgeoning empire.

A key element in fueling Amazon's ascent was its strategic navigation of the U.S. tax code. For instance, in 2018, despite reporting over $11 billion in profits before taxes, Amazon's meticulous financial planning resulted in $0 federal income tax liability, even securing a $129 million tax rebate. This financial maneuvering wasn't exploitation but a testament to the power of understanding and aligning with tax incentives designed to stimulate investment and innovation. Amazon's adept use of carryforward losses from its earlier, leaner years, alongside deductions for substantial investments in research and development (R&D) and stock-based employee compensation, exemplifies strategic tax planning at its finest.

This approach enabled Amazon to price its offerings competitively, innovate aggressively, and expand rapidly—outcomes that would have been markedly slower without such nuanced financial strategies. Amazon's journey from a garage to global dominance underscores the profound impact that strategic tax planning and reinvestment can have on business growth and development.

For individual investors and entrepreneurs, Amazon's blueprint offers invaluable lessons on the importance of strategic tax planning. Leveraging tax incentives, deductions, and credits allows for the conservation of resources, which can then be redirected towards growth and expansion efforts. This strategy doesn't just maximize financial potential; it catalyzes compounded growth, setting the stage for long-term success and innovation.

Amazon's origin story and meteoric rise serve as a playbook for aspiring entrepreneurs and investors. It highlights the power of starting small, the courage to dream big, and the strategic acumen to navigate the complex landscape of taxes and investments—a true testament to the enduring impact of foresight, innovation, delayed gratification and meticulous planning.

FOUNDATIONAL PRINCIPALS FOR TAX SAAVY INVESTORS

Before we unpack the most advanced tax strategies employed by the wealthy, it's vital to embrace and internalize two foundational principals:

Principal #1: It's Not Uncle Sam's Money, it's Yours.

In a democratic society, the money you earn and the wealth you build unequivocally belong to you. While taxes are a necessary means of supporting public services like infrastructure, defense, and education, it's essential to remember that your financial resources are fundamentally yours to manage.

Principal #2: The Tax Law Is Mostly About Reducing Your Taxes

Contrary to common misconceptions, tax laws are not intended to burden individuals with excessive taxes. In fact, the primary purpose of tax legislation is to empower you to reduce your tax liability, not to increase it. In the tax code of over 6000 pages, only 30 pages are about raising taxes, while the remainder is about reducing them. Understanding this core principle is the first step toward effectively navigating the tax landscape.

Principal #3: You are the only one responsible for your taxes.

Who is responsible for paying your taxes? You are, of course. That also means that you are the only person responsible for planning and implementing your tax strategies. Taking ownership in this is essential.

You, and only you, have the power and control over your money and your taxes. Nobody else. Those who do not take ownership over their tax planning think, "My tax advisor handles my taxes." But this is a myth that needs clarification. Your tax advisor can't handle your taxes in the sense of taking proactive steps to reduce them. They can prepare your tax returns, provide advice on specific situations, and perhaps even educate you of rules that could affect your taxes. But they cannot take the actual steps to reduce your taxes. Only you can do that. You still need a competent Tax Advisor on your team, but don’t relay on them to make your dreams come true.

This principle reinforces the importance of being actively involved in your financial planning, especially when it comes to taxes. It's about taking ownership of your financial future. Understanding the tax code, the available strategies, and how to apply them in your situation requires intentionality on your part.

Strategic tax planning is not a passive process but an active, ongoing endeavor. Over time you become more and more empowered to make informed decisions, leveraging the advice of professionals but always taking the final steps yourself. This proactive approach not only helps you minimize your tax liability but also enhances your ability to build and protect your wealth over time.

With these foundational truths firmly established, you're better prepared to explore the specific tax strategies that can help you build and safeguard your wealth.

Now instead of giving every single tax strategy available, (many of which we coach our clients through in our Tax Free Investor's Club) through the rest of this chapter I will focus on only the most powerful tax strategies.

TAX STRATEGIES FOR SAAVY INVESTORS

THE UNMATCHED POWER OF ACCELERATED DEPRECIATION IN MULTI-FAMILY REAL ESTATE

Cost segregation stands as the single most powerful tax strategy for real estate investors seeking to maximize their investment's profitability. This secret weapon propels the most successful portfolios to staggering heights of profitability and tax efficiency. This strategy, leveraged by billionaires and savvy investors alike, is none other than accelerated depreciation through cost segregation. It's not just a tax strategy; it's a bold statement on smart investing that distinguishes the truly informed investor from the rest.

THE BILLIONAIRE'S PLAYBOOK: ACCELERATED DEPRECIATION

Imagine having the ability to legally fast-track your investment returns while simultaneously reducing your tax obligations. This is the essence of accelerated depreciation, a cornerstone in the billionaire's investment playbook. It's a method that, when applied with precision and strategic insight, transforms your real estate assets into vehicles of unparalleled tax savings and cash flow enhancement.

HOW ACCELERATED DEPRECIATION WORKS

At its core, accelerated depreciation via cost segregation is a meticulous process of dissecting a property purchase into various components, some of which can depreciate much faster than the standard 27.5 years for residential rental property. This reclassification into 5, 7, or 15-year categories dramatically increases your depreciation deductions in the initial years of ownership, effectively reducing taxable income and bolstering your investment's cash flow.

A PRACTICAL ILLUSTRATION

Consider the transformative impact of accelerated depreciation with a tangible example: a $13.9 million multi-family property undergoes a strategic cost segregation study. The study results in significant portions of the property being reclassified into faster-depreciating categories, thereby shifting a standard annual depreciation of $311,981.14 to an astounding $4,543,986.65 in the first year alone. For an investor holding a 7.19% stake, this strategy elevates their share of depreciation from $22,444.69 to $326,905.53, marking a monumental leap in tax efficiency and investment liquidity.

THE ROLE OF THE GENERAL PARTNER (GP) TEAM

Navigating the complexities of accelerated depreciation demands more than just a passing familiarity with tax codes—it requires the guidance of a seasoned General Partner (GP) team. This team becomes your beacon through the intricate landscape of real estate investment, ensuring that every step, from the feasibility analysis of a cost segregation study to the meticulous documentation required, is handled with expertise and strategic foresight. Their role is to demystify the process, aligning your investment with the pathways tread by the most successful investors.

Here are actionable insights to guide you moving forward:

1. **Partner with Expertise:** Seek out GP teams with a proven track record in navigating cost segregation and accelerated depreciation strategies.

2. **Educate Yourself:** Understanding the mechanics of your investment strategies empowers you to make informed

decisions.

3. **Document Rigorously:** Meticulous documentation not only facilitates tax compliance but also maximizes your investment's financial performance.

4. **Stay Informed:** Tax laws evolve, and so should your strategies. Keeping abreast of legislative changes ensures your investments remain optimally positioned for tax efficiency.

The strategic use of accelerated depreciation in multi-family real estate investment is more than a tax strategy; it's a profound opportunity to reshape your financial future. It's a testament to the power of knowledge, strategy, and the right partnerships in unlocking the full potential of your investments. Inspired by the practices of the most successful investors, this approach invites you to not just grow your wealth but to do so with an eye towards innovation, efficiency, and the enduring principles of smart investing. Embrace this path, and you align yourself with the visionaries who see beyond the horizon, turning real estate into a bastion of financial growth and tax efficiency.

THE LONG-TERM IMPACT OF 1031 EXCHANGES

In the realm of real estate investment, few strategies stand the test of time like the 1031 exchange. Often hailed as the investor's secret weapon, this provision of the Internal Revenue Code offers a pathway to defer capital gains taxes on the sale of investment properties, unlocking a world of possibilities for long-term wealth accumulation and portfolio growth.

THE FOUNDATION OF WEALTH PRESERVATION

At its core, the 1031 exchange empowers investors to defer capital gains taxes by reinvesting proceeds from the sale of one property into a like-kind replacement property. This seemingly simple maneuver, when executed strategically, lays the groundwork for preserving and compounding wealth over the long term.

A LONG-TERM PERSPECTIVE

Consider the implications of a well-crafted 1031 exchange not just on a single property sale, but on the entire trajectory of your investment portfolio over the next several decades. By deferring taxes today, investors gain access to additional capital that can be reinvested into higher-yielding properties, thereby accelerating portfolio growth and wealth accumulation.

THE POWER OF DEFERRED TAXES

One of the most compelling aspects of the 1031 exchange is its ability to defer taxes indefinitely, provided investors continue to utilize this strategy with each subsequent property sale. This means that instead of paying taxes on capital gains today, investors can leverage those funds to acquire larger, more lucrative properties, fueling exponential portfolio expansion.

KICK THE BUCKET DOWN THE ROAD

It's important to recognize that while the 1031 exchange offers significant tax benefits, it doesn't eliminate taxes altogether. Instead, it effectively kicks the bucket down the road, deferring taxes to a later date. However, when executed strategically, this deferral can have profound implications for long-term wealth accumulation, allowing investors to maximize the value of their investment portfolios over time.

COMPOUNDING WEALTH THROUGH STRATEGIC REINVESTMENT

Imagine the scenario: with each successful 1031 exchange, your investment portfolio grows in both size and profitability. The capital gains taxes that would have been owed on each property sale are instead reinvested into new assets, compounding your wealth over time. This compounding effect, when compounded over multiple investment cycles, can lead to exponential portfolio growth and financial security.

SAFEGUARDING YOUR LEGACY

Beyond the immediate benefits of tax deferral and portfolio growth, the 1031 exchange offers a powerful tool for safeguarding your legacy. By deferring taxes on property sales, investors can preserve more of their wealth to pass on to future generations, ensuring a lasting impact that transcends individual investments.

NAVIGATING THE COMPLEXITIES

While the concept of the 1031 exchange may seem straightforward, navigating its nuances and intricacies requires a thorough understanding of tax laws and real estate investment strategies. Partnering with experienced professionals who specialize in 1031 exchanges can provide invaluable guidance and ensure that your long-term financial goals are met with precision and efficiency.

SETTING UP YOUR ENTITY CORRECTLY

In real estate, the bold decision of entity structure is not just paperwork—it's the secret weapon that elevates you from the crowd to the summit of investment mastery. This path to greatness echoes the timeless strategy of Andrew Carnegie, who masterfully advised, "own nothing, control everything." Embodying this wisdom through careful entity selection, strategic tax planning, and the judicious use of holding companies for maintaining anonymity lays the foundation of a real estate empire of unparalleled strength and resilience.

1. STRATEGICALLY SELECTING THE RIGHT BUSINESS ENTITY

In aligning with Carnegie's timeless strategy, the decision of which business entity to utilize in your real estate endeavors is foundational. This choice should reflect your goals for liability protection, tax efficiency, and operational flexibility.

- **Limited Liability Companies (LLCs)** emerge as the premier choice for embodying Carnegie's principle. By holding real estate investments within an LLC, investors can enjoy the benefits of asset protection and pass-through taxation, effectively separating personal assets from business liabilities while ensuring profits are only taxed once at the personal level.

- **S Corporations**, although restrictive in terms of shareholder qualifications and passive loss deductions, offer a structured way to manage active real estate businesses, enabling salary and dividend payments that could lead to potential tax savings under the right circumstances.

- **C Corporations** serve a specific niche within real estate investment strategies, particularly for operations focusing on capital-intensive ventures where double taxation can be mitigated through business reinvestment and strategic planning.

2. LEVERAGING TAX DEDUCTIONS AND REAL ESTATE PROFESSIONAL STATUS (REPS)

To fully embrace the "control everything" aspect of Carnegie's strategy, optimizing tax deductions through careful planning and potentially qualifying for Real Estate Professional Status are crucial steps. These measures not only reduce taxable income but also align with the proactive management and strategic control over one's real estate investments.

3. MASTERING ANONYMITY AND ASSET PROTECTION THROUGH A HOLDING COMPANY LLC

A Holding Company LLC established in a state renowned for its stance on anonymity, such as Delaware, Nevada, or Wyoming, plays a pivotal role in the "own nothing" facet of Carnegie's advice. This structure offers:

- **Anonymity**: By avoiding personal identifiers in the LLC name, employing a registered agent, and using a non-personal address, investors can maintain a degree of separation between their personal identity and their investment activities.

- **Asset Protection**: The use of a holding company to own interests in other LLCs that directly hold real estate not only compartmentalizes liability but also reinforces the principle of controlling assets without direct ownership, thus limiting personal exposure.

4. OPERATIONAL EXCELLENCE AND COMPLIANCE

In this structure, operational diligence and adherence to compliance standards are paramount. Proper documentation, accounting practices, and legal formalities must be meticulously maintained to uphold the integrity and benefits of the chosen entity structures. This operational discipline ensures that the investor can effectively control their real estate portfolio, maximize benefits, and navigate the complexities of real estate investment with strategic acumen.

SEGMENT YOUR PORTFOLIO FOR PROTECTION, EFFICIENCY, AND TAX OPTIMIZATION

"Investing in real estate is a craft where structure meets strategy, amplifying your gains through meticulous tax planning." Within the protective canopy of your Holding Company LLC, tailoring your investment structures to the unique contours of your portfolio not only streamlines management but also unveils significant tax advantages. By segmenting your investments into distinct LLCs for different types of real estate activities or markets, you not only safeguard your assets but also craft a finely tuned tax strategy that aligns with your financial goals.

- **Fix and Flips**: Establishing a dedicated LLC for your fix and flip projects isolates these transaction-heavy activities from your other investments, enabling focused tax planning around these operations. This structure allows for the direct offset of expenses against revenues generated from flips, optimizing tax deductions related to renovations, marketing, and sale expenses, and ensuring that the gains are taxed in the most favorable manner under current tax laws.

- **Rental Properties**: By grouping rental properties under a separate LLC, you leverage the tax benefits of long-term investment strategies, including depreciation, maintenance expenses, and interest deductions. This separation aids in navigating the passive activity loss rules and real estate professional status, potentially unlocking the ability to offset passive income losses against other forms of income, thus reducing overall tax liability.

- **Geographical or Market Segmentation**: Creating separate LLCs for investments in different states or markets allows you to adapt to the varying tax laws and incentives of each jurisdiction. This not only ensures compliance but also maximizes local tax benefits, credits, and deductions available to real estate investors, tailoring your tax strategy to the nuances of each location.

- **Large Commercial Investments**: Allocating each significant commercial investment to its own LLC facilitates targeted tax planning for large-scale ventures. This includes leveraging cost segregation studies to accelerate depreciation, capturing tax credits specific to commercial developments, and managing property tax strategies effectively. Each property's financials are cleanly segmented, simplifying tax reporting and enhancing the precision of tax optimization strategies.

CRAFTING A TAX-EFFICIENT EMPIRE UNDER THE AUSPICES OF YOUR HOLDING COMPANY

"Through strategic segmentation, each investment becomes a cog in a well-oiled tax-saving machine." This advanced structuring under your Holding Company LLC does more than protect—it strategically positions each segment of your real estate portfolio for optimal tax efficiency. By isolating different types of real estate activities, you not only fine-tune your tax strategy to each investment's specific circumstances but also create a flexible framework that can adapt to tax law changes, maximizing your after-tax returns.

Incorporating this level of tax strategic planning into your real estate investment approach transforms your holdings into a dynamic ecosystem of efficiently managed assets. This ecosystem not only stands resilient in the face of liability and market volatility but also thrives under a tailored tax strategy that propels your investments towards greater profitability and growth. Through this meticulous alignment of entity structuring and tax planning, you pave the path to a real estate legacy characterized by both formidable asset protection and profound tax efficiency.

INCORPORATE TAX STRATEGY ACROSS YOUR REAL ESTATE PORTFOLIO

If you're an investor leveraging a blend of fix and flips, rental properties, and commercial investments, you're positioning yourself to take advantage of a diverse real estate portfolio that can optimize returns and minimize tax liabilities. Here's how to strategically navigate the tax implications of each investment type to enhance your overall financial performance:

FIX AND FLIPS: MANAGING CAPITAL GAINS

Fix and flips often result in significant capital gains due to the short-term nature of these investments. These gains are taxed at a higher rate than long-term investments, potentially increasing your tax liability for the year.

Strategic Counsel:

- **Timing Your Sales**: Consider the timing of your fix and flip sales. Delaying a sale to the next tax year can help manage your tax liabilities, especially if you anticipate a lower income year.

- **Reinvesting Profits**: Reinvest profits from fix and flips into longer-term investments, like rental properties or commercial real estate, which offer depreciation benefits and can offset the higher tax rate on short-term capital gains.

RENTAL PROPERTIES: LEVERAGING DEPRECIATION

Rental properties provide a steady stream of passive income and the benefit of depreciation, which can offset the income generated by the property, reducing your overall taxable income.

Strategic Counsel:

-

Maximize Depreciation: Ensure you're maximizing your depreciation deductions on rental properties. This is crucial for offsetting the income from rentals and can also mitigate the tax impact of your fix and flip gains.

- **Passive Activity Losses**: If you qualify as a Real Estate Professional, you can deduct losses from rental activities against other income, which is especially valuable in high capital gains tax years from fix and flips.

COMMERCIAL INVESTMENTS: UTILIZING COST SEGREGATION

Investing in commercial real estate, especially multifamily properties, allows for the utilization of cost segregation studies to accelerate depreciation deductions. This strategy is powerful for reducing taxable income in the year of investment.

Strategic Counsel:

- **Cost Segregation Study**: After acquiring a new commercial property, conduct a cost segregation study to identify personal property components and land improvements that can be depreciated over a shorter period, providing substantial upfront deductions.

- **Bonus Depreciation**: Take advantage of bonus depreciation rules that allow for immediate deduction of a percentage of the cost of qualifying assets in the first year of service, further reducing taxable income.

INTEGRATING STRATEGIES FOR OPTIMAL TAX EFFICIENCY

As an investor engaging in fix and flips, rental properties, and commercial investments, your goal should be to integrate these strategies in a manner that balances income generation with tax minimization:

1. **Use fix and flip profits to invest in rental and commercial properties**. This not only diversifies your portfolio but also provides opportunities to reduce the tax impact through depreciation and cost segregation.

2. **Leverage the passive income and depreciation from rental properties** to offset the taxes on the gains from fix and flips. Consider structuring your investments so that rental losses can be used most effectively.

3. **Capitalize on the tax benefits of commercial real estate investments**. The accelerated and bonus depreciation from these investments can significantly reduce your overall taxable income, which is particularly useful in years where you realize substantial capital gains from fix and flips.

4. **Maintain a holistic view of your portfolio**. Work with a tax advisor who specializes in real estate to plan your sales, purchases, and renovations strategically. This professional can help you time your investments to optimize tax advantages across your entire portfolio.

5. **Diversify a Portion with a Self-Directed IRA**: For a portion of all your fix and flips, consider using a Self-Directed Individual Retirement Account (SDIRA). By flipping

properties within an SDIRA, you can avoid capital gains taxes on those houses, as the profits will be sheltered within the retirement account. This can significantly minimize your capital gains tax liability, but be mindful of the rules and restrictions governing real estate investments in IRAs.

6. **Implement the BRRRR Method**: Instead of selling your flip properties immediately after renovation, explore the Buy, Rehab, Rent, Refinance, Repeat (BRRRR) method. By refinancing the property after rehabbing and renting it out, you can pull out your initial investment capital without incurring a tax burden on that cash-out. This strategy not only defers taxes but also allows you to keep the property as a source of ongoing rental income.

7. **Refinance and Rent Before Selling**: In rapidly appreciating markets, consider refinancing and renting out the property for at least two years before selling. This approach allows you to capitalize on market growth, potentially increasing the property's equity. The cash-out refinance can provide liquidity without immediate tax implications, and renting the property can offer additional income and tax benefits, such as depreciation. After two years, you may also qualify for the Section 121 exclusion if you decide to sell, which can further minimize your tax burden.

8. **Keep meticulous records and plan for the future**. Detailed record-keeping not only supports your tax filing but also aids in strategic planning. Forecasting your income and taxes can help you make informed decisions about when to sell, hold, or acquire new properties.

By thoughtfully integrating these strategies, you can create a real estate portfolio that not only maximizes your income and growth potential but also strategically manages your tax liabilities, enhancing your overall financial success in the realm of real estate investing.

LEGACY BUILDING WITH LIVING TRUSTS

Imagine a world where your real estate legacy lives on, untouched by the hands of time and tax collectors. This isn't just a dream—it's a reality crafted through the strategic use of living trusts." As real estate investors, we're not just building portfolios; we're creating legacies. And in this journey, understanding the power of living trusts becomes our beacon of wisdom, guiding us towards a future where our investments continue to flourish, even in our absence.

Living trusts are more than mere legal documents; they are vessels carrying your vision into the future. They ensure that the wealth you amass through diligent investing and sharp strategy is preserved and passed down exactly as you envision. "Control everything, own nothing," as the adage goes, resonates deeply here. By placing your real estate assets into a living trust, you maintain control over your investments while securing their passage to your beneficiaries without the public spectacle and delays of probate.

CRAFTING YOUR FINANCIAL MASTERPIECE

Privacy and the Path to Prosperity: In the realm of real estate investment, privacy is a treasure. Living trusts shield the details of your estate from public eyes, keeping your financial affairs as confidential as your strategies. This privacy ensures that your legacy is distributed according to your wishes, safeguarding your family's future and the fruits of your labor.

A Symphony of Strategic Control: The true mastery of a real estate investor lies in the ability to direct the future from the present. Living trusts offer you the baton to conduct how and when your assets are distributed, allowing you to orchestrate a legacy that echoes your values, whether that's providing for loved ones, setting the stage for future generations, or fueling philanthropic endeavors.

The Blueprint for Continuity and Protection: Unforeseen circumstances can bring a halt to even the most meticulously planned investments. Living trusts serve as a blueprint for continuity, ensuring that your investments remain operational and in trusted hands if you're unable to oversee them yourself. Moreover, they can offer a shield, protecting your beneficiaries' inheritances from potential creditors and claimants, ensuring that your legacy is used as you intended.

BEYOND THE HORIZON: TAX EFFICIENCY AND ESTATE PLANNING

While living trusts in themselves do not directly mitigate tax liabilities, their strategic application can lead to significant estate tax benefits, especially when employing irrevocable trusts. These structures can effectively remove assets from your estate, potentially lowering estate taxes and maximizing what your heirs receive. It's a horizon worth exploring, where the culmination of your investment savvy and strategic foresight can yield a legacy unburdened by unnecessary tax implications.

THE HIGH COST OF PROBATE

Probate is the legal process through which a deceased person's estate is properly distributed to heirs and designated beneficiaries and any debt owed to creditors is paid off. While necessary, probate can be a lengthy and expensive process, with costs that can significantly erode your estate's value.

Financial Implications: The costs associated with probate can vary widely depending on the complexity and size of the estate, as well as the jurisdiction. However, it's not uncommon for probate fees (including court fees, executor's fees, attorney's fees, and appraisal costs) to range from 2% to 7% of the estate's total value. For a real estate portfolio valued at $1 million, this could mean $20,000 to $70,000 lost to probate costs alone.

Time Delays: Beyond the financial costs, probate can be a slow process, often taking anywhere from six months to several years to complete. During this time, your heirs may not have access to the assets they need or wish to sell, and real estate holdings may not be managed as effectively as you would have managed them, potentially leading to a decrease in value.

THE STRATEGIC ADVANTAGE OF AVOIDING PROBATE

"Avoiding probate is akin to a masterful move that safeguards your estate from unnecessary erosion while ensuring your legacy is passed on swiftly and according to your wishes."

Immediate Transfer of Assets: By utilizing a living trust, your real estate investments and other assets can bypass the probate process entirely, allowing for an immediate transfer to your beneficiaries upon your passing. This swift transition can be critical for maintaining the value and operational integrity of your real estate holdings.

Preserving Estate Value: Avoiding probate saves potentially tens of thousands of dollars—or more—in fees, preserving the full value of your estate for your heirs. In the context of real estate investing, this means more capital for your beneficiaries to invest, grow, or live on, in accordance with your legacy plans.

Maintaining Privacy: Probate is a public process, meaning the details of your estate, including the value of your real estate holdings, become a matter of public record. A living trust, on the other hand, ensures that your estate remains a private affair, keeping your financial matters confidential and out of the public eye.

ACTIONABLE STEPS FOR REAL ESTATE INVESTORS

1. **Establish a Living Trust**: Consult with an estate planning attorney to establish a living trust that includes all your real estate investments. This will allow these assets to pass directly to your beneficiaries without going through probate.

2. **Regularly Review and Update Your Trust**: As your real estate portfolio grows and changes, make sure your living trust reflects these changes. Regular reviews ensure that

newly acquired properties are included in the trust and that your estate plan remains aligned with your current wishes.

3. **Educate Your Heirs**: Make sure your beneficiaries understand the structure and benefits of the living trust, as well as their roles and responsibilities. Education is key to ensuring a smooth transition when the time comes.

ENVISIONING YOUR LEGACY

As you stand at the helm of your real estate empire, consider how a living trust can anchor your legacy in stability and intention. The structures you choose—be they revocable for flexibility or irrevocable for tax advantages—should mirror the vision you have for your estate. Partner with estate planning experts who understand the intricacies of real estate investments to tailor a plan that reflects your ambitions and safeguards your legacy.

"In every property acquired, every deal closed, and every strategy executed lies a brushstroke in the masterpiece of your legacy." Let living trusts be the canvas upon which your masterpiece is preserved, protecting and perpetuating your impact on the world. This is the essence of true wealth and success in real estate investment—not merely in accumulating assets but in ensuring they serve your higher purpose, today, tomorrow, and beyond your lifetime.

Embrace the power of living trusts in your estate planning. In doing so, you not only secure your legacy but also inspire a future where your investments continue to thrive, a testament to the enduring impact of strategic foresight and meticulous planning in the world of real estate.

PART 4: LONG-TERM PLANNING

NINE

WEALTH PRESERVATION

Wealth preservation is not merely a strategy; it is the peak of financial wisdom. This statement encapsulates the profound shift experienced by those who have successfully navigated the tumultuous waters of wealth accumulation. It marks the transition from a phase of aggressive growth to one of deliberate safeguarding and stewardship. This chapter delves into the essence of this shift—a transformation that signifies not just financial success but the dawn of a new era in personal and familial wealth management.

For many individuals, the journey towards wealth preservation begins when their net worth crosses a certain threshold. This figure varies significantly from one person to another, symbolizing a personal victory and the culmination of years of strategic investment, calculated risks, and moments of serendipity. For others, the transition is less about the numbers and more about a change in life's seasons. As the years advance, the priority shifts from expansion to ensuring that the wealth amassed will benefit not just the current generation but those yet to come.

This shift is not an ending but a commencement. It represents a stage where the focus turns to securing a legacy, employing strategies that aim for the longevity and sustainability of one’s financial impact. It is in this phase that generational wealth takes form, crafted with foresight and a deep understanding of the importance of preservation.

Transitioning from building to preserving wealth is as much a shift in mindset as it is in strategy. It is a reflection of your journey, a marker of the intelligent decisions and risks undertaken over time. But more profoundly, it is a move towards greater wisdom—the realization that the true value of wealth is not in its mere accumulation but in its capacity to ensure security, opportunity, and prosperity for future generations.

This chapter is designed to guide you through this critical transition, providing insights into the methodologies that safeguard financial legacies. Whether this phase is heralded by reaching certain net worth milestones or by the natural progression of life, moving from building to preserving wealth is a pivotal moment. It is an opportunity to reflect, plan, and act with wisdom, setting the stage for a legacy that extends beyond mere numbers. Welcome to the nuanced art and science of wealth preservation.

THE SAFETY AND POWER OF DEBT FUNDS

Real Estate backed Debt Funds stand as a beacon of stability in the turbulent sea of investment options, offering a safe harbor for those seeking to balance the promise of real estate with the desire for risk mitigation. Choosing to invest in these funds is not just a strategic decision; it's a commitment to safeguarding one’s financial future with a method that has been meticulously crafted for security.

Central to the appeal of Real Estate backed Debt Funds is their inherently low-risk nature. By pooling capital to lend money secured by real estate, these funds create a unique investment proposition that combines the tangible asset security of real estate with the predictable, fixed-income characteristics of a debt instrument. This fusion presents a compelling case for investors, particularly those cautious about the volatility and complexities associated with direct property ownership.

The security embedded in these Debt Funds comes from the loans being backed by physical properties. This means that should a borrower fail to meet their obligations, the fund, acting on behalf of its investors, holds a secured interest in the real estate asset. This collateral serves as a significant risk mitigator, ensuring that even in the event of a default, there is a tangible asset to recover funds from. This layer of protection is a critical factor that distinguishes Real Estate backed Debt Funds as a lower-risk investment compared to many other options in the market.

Furthermore, the structured nature of these investments—wherein funds are lent out at fixed interest rates—provides a steady, predictable flow of income. This predictability is a hallmark of a safe investment, offering clarity and peace of mind to investors who prioritize stability over speculative gains. The ability to generate consistent returns, regardless of the broader market's ups and downs, positions these Debt Funds as an ideal choice for those with a risk-averse profile or those looking to diversify their portfolios with a more secure asset class.

Real Estate backed Debt Funds are, therefore, not just about tapping into the wealth-building potential of real estate; they're about doing so in a manner that prioritizes safety and low risk. They embody a prudent approach to investment, where the goal is not merely growth but sustainable, secure growth that can withstand market fluctuations.

This investment strategy resonates deeply with those who view financial stewardship as a duty to protect and preserve wealth. By aligning with Real Estate backed Debt Funds, investors embrace a path that leads not just to potential financial gains but to peace of mind, knowing their investment is built on a foundation of safety and strategic foresight.

TEN

TRUE WEALTH: GENEROSITY & LEGACY

I was in a cigar lounge in Manhattan, just killing time before my flight home, enjoying a peaceful moment by the windows with a view of Central Park. As I lit up a Churchill, I ended up chatting with another guy across the room who was also into real estate. During our talk, I noticed he had tattoos of 6 little footprints running down his arm.

Curious, I asked him about the tattoos, and he explained that each one was for each of his six kids. That got us talking about our families. I shared that my wife and I already had five kids, and I was on the fence about having another one, even though she really wanted a sixth.

When I told him about my situation, he got up, came over to shake my hand, and said, "Out of everything we've talked about today — **that is true wealth, my brother.**"

That comment really resonated with me. I thought about it the whole flight home. It reminded me that my family is not just the reason for building wealth but is the real wealth itself.

So, when I finally got back home and shared the whole story with my wife, including how I was feeling about everything. After I told her I was finally ready to try for baby number six with her, she looked at me with this big grin and said, "Well, you better be ready, because I'm pregnant!"

MONEY VERSUS WEALTH

Money is the currency of necessity; it's the tool we use to navigate the day-to-day demands of living, from paying bills to securing our immediate comforts and pleasures. It's tangible, often fleeting, and closely tied to the present moment—serving as a means to fulfill our current needs and desires. Money fuels our ability to have experiences, creating memories with those we love, and provides a sense of security in the immediacy of life's demands. It's the financial response to the question of how we maintain our daily lives and afford the experiences that bring us joy and satisfaction.

Wealth, on the other hand, transcends the immediacy of paying bills and indulging in experiences. It embodies a broader, more profound purpose that extends beyond the self. Wealth is something beyond our little self-centered worlds, and it has the power to impact lives beyond our own, serving as a vessel for generosity, impact, and legacy. It's not merely about possessing financial abundance but about what we can do with that abundance to influence the world and the lives of others positively. Wealth is the capacity to extend our reach, to contribute to the well-being of future generations, and to invest in the betterment of the world around us.

WEALTH IS FOR GENEROSITY

Would you rather receive help without the capacity to repay that person, or would you rather be the person that gives the help? The adage that it is better to give than to receive speaks volumes about the essence of true wealth. This introduces a profound question: What if we began to measure our wealth not by the millions we make per year nor by our assets, but by how much we give away each year? Consider the remarkable example of David Green, who is said to give away a billion per year, setting a precedent for generosity that transcends traditional measures of wealth.

Embracing this paradigm shift, we see generosity not just as an act but as the defining principle of true wealth. It challenges us to see our resources as streams of potential, flowing outward to quench the thirst of communities and initiatives in need. This perspective reframes our understanding of value, encouraging us to use our abundance to empower, educate, and uplift, thereby enriching not just our lives but those of others.

The ripple effect of generosity extends beyond the initial act, embodying the true essence of impact. Each act of kindness, each investment in another's future, initiates a cascade of positive change that can reshape communities. By recognizing our capacity for influence, we're encouraged to cast our stones of generosity into humanity's vast pond, knowing the ripples will carry far and wide, perpetuating cycles of kindness and support.

Influence through generosity is built on empathy, contrasting sharply with traditional notions of authority. This form of influence, rooted in prioritizing the well-being of others, forges connections based on mutual respect and shared purpose. Such leadership inspires, motivates, and unites, proving that the most profound authority comes from our ability to serve and uplift.

Authenticity is crucial to meaningful giving, ensuring our acts of generosity resonate with our deepest values and beliefs. When we give in a way that reflects our true selves, we create lasting connections. This authenticity turns our generosity into a powerful expression of our identity, leaving an indelible mark on the world.

The harmony between giving and receiving is essential, underscoring the interconnectedness of generosity. Welcoming the gratitude and support we receive in return enriches our capacity to give, ensuring our wellspring of generosity remains vibrant. This balance keeps the cycle of generosity alive, allowing us to continue making an impact with a replenished spirit.

Imagine a world where wealth is measured by generosity rather than assets. Figures like David Green inspire us not by the wealth they accumulate but by the billions they give away each year. That's my aim. This shift in perspective is both a privilege and a call to action, stirring within us a desire to contribute to something greater than ourselves. The delight of giving, of being part of initiatives that uplift humanity, transcends any form of recognition, committing us to serve the needy, the poor, the helpless, driven by the pure joy of making a difference.

By integrating these concepts into our lives, generosity becomes not just an action but a fundamental aspect of our existence. It compels us to view our wealth as a tool for collective betterment, crafting a legacy defined not by what we accumulate but by the lives we touch and the worlds we transform. Through generosity, we discover the true essence of wealth: the power to create a legacy of positive change that endures beyond our time, measured not in dollars but in the depth of our impact and the lives we uplift.

WEALTH IS FOR MAKING A DIFFERENCE

At the heart of Impact Investment Partners we have a commitment that stretches beyond the conventional pursuit of wealth. Our business model, focused on flipping apartment complexes over 3-5 year periods, is fundamentally driven by a mission to create impactful change. This approach is a living embodiment of the Triple Bottom Line—prioritizing people, planet, and profit. Through our contributions to organizations like Techo in Latin America, we not only see returns on investments but also participate in building homes and supporting communities, showcasing how profit can coexist with purpose.

Our dedication to the 'People' aspect of the Triple Bottom Line has inspired the creation of Fire Nights, a nonprofit initiative aimed at fostering a movement of men across the United States towards better mental health and healthier relationships. Fire Nights stands as a testament to our belief that investing in people's well-being is the foundation of creating lasting impact. This initiative reflects our commitment to enriching lives, not just through physical infrastructure but by nurturing the mental and emotional health of individuals, thereby strengthening the very fabric of our communities.

Expanding Perspectives Beyond Profit

The journey to true wealth requires a shift in perspective, from a singular focus on profits to a holistic view that equally values social and environmental returns. The Triple Bottom Line encourages us to consider how our investments and business activities affect not only our financial bottom line but also the well-being of people and the health of our planet. This broader approach to success challenges us to innovate and operate in ways that contribute positively to society and the environment while still achieving economic viability.

Strategic Impact Through Operational Efficiency

Efficiency in business is not merely about maximizing profits; it's about amplifying impact. By leveraging our operational strengths for philanthropic endeavors, such as our work with Fire Nights, we demonstrate how optimized processes and strategic thinking can extend the reach and effectiveness of our efforts to make a difference. This efficiency enables us to touch more lives and create a broader impact, proving that the principles of business can be seamlessly integrated with the goals of philanthropy.

Global Actions with Local Resonance

Our global reach provides us with a unique opportunity to address complex challenges across borders. By adopting a global perspective, we can implement initiatives that have a profound local impact, from environmental sustainability projects to health and education reforms. This approach showcases the power of thinking globally while acting locally, ensuring that our efforts to drive positive change are felt deeply within the communities we aim to support.

Fostering Collaborations for Collective Impact

True change is a collective endeavor. By partnering with governments, non-profits, and the private sector, we can create synergies that amplify the impact of our initiatives. These collaborative efforts exemplify the strength of unity in pursuit of a common goal, enabling us to tackle societal challenges more effectively and efficiently. Through partnerships, we can pool resources, share expertise, and multiply the positive outcomes of our actions.

Redefining Success through the Triple Bottom Line

Our engagement with Impact Investment Partners and the establishment of Fire Nights embody the essence of the Triple Bottom Line, setting a new standard for measuring success. By integrating this holistic approach into our wealth planning and business strategies, we inspire others to consider how their actions can foster not just economic growth but also social progress and environmental sustainability. This shift towards impact-focused planning paves the way for a legacy of positive change, where true wealth is gauged by the breadth and depth of our contributions to the world.

ELEVEN

YOUR PERSONALIZED 20-YEAR ROADMAP

In ancient China, one of my favorite stories unfolds revealing the power of long-term thinking and simple compounding decisions. This tale begins with a wise man who introduced the emperor to the game of chess, a game that intrigued and delighted the ruler. In return for this gift, the wise man asked for a seemingly modest reward: a single grain of rice placed on the first square of the chessboard, and then that the grain of rice would double on each subsequent square.

Amused by such a humble request, the emperor quickly agreed, unaware of the lesson he was about to learn. The first few squares seemed inconsequential—a grain of rice became two, then four, then eight. But as the servants continued doubling the grains across the chessboard, the numbers grew exponentially.

By the halfway point of the chessboard, the emperor began to realize the gravity of his promise. The palace's granaries started to deplete as the wise man's reward transformed from a small pile of rice into mountains of grains. By the 64th square, the total amount required was a staggering 18,446,744,073,709,551,615 grains of rice—far more than existed in the entire kingdom.

This ancient parable illuminates the incredible power of the compound effect. It shows how small, consistent actions, when doubled and redoubled over time, can lead to outcomes beyond our wildest dreams. As you stand at the threshold of planning the next 20 years of your life, let this story be the wind in your sail.

Just like the grains of rice on the chessboard, the decisions you make and the actions you take today may seem small or insignificant. Yet, compounded over two decades, these choices have the potential to grow into a life of unparalleled richness and achievement.

This tale teaches us not to underestimate the power of starting small. As you lay the foundation for your future, remember that every giant leap begins with a single, small step. And with each step doubled in effort, commitment, and learning, you're not just moving towards your goals—you're accelerating towards a future that exceeds your imagination.

Let the wisdom of the wise man and the oversight of the emperor guide you as you embark on this 20-year journey. Embrace compounded consistent decisions, and watch as the seemingly modest investments of your today transform into the extraordinary achievements of your tomorrow.

STEP ONE: ENVISION YOUR FUTURE WITHOUT LIMITS

As you begin to plan out your future, especially through real estate investment, the first and perhaps most crucial step is to allow yourself to dream—dream big, dream boldly, and dream without any limits. This is not about setting realistic expectations or goals based on your current situation. It's about imagining a future that stretches beyond your wildest expectations. It's about envisioning a life that's not just better but is the epitome of what you've always hoped for and beyond.

Imagine it. This is serious. Right now, put this book down and close your eyes. Try to imagine your ideal life 20 years from now. Do not pull this book back up until you've seriously tried to imagine it.

Now try to 10x that dream. You're probably thinking that I'm insane, but this is a proven stratefy. This pushes you to think bigger and beyond the conventional. If you aim for an outcome ten times greater than what you consider achievable, you're setting a course that challenges you to think differently, work smarter, and relentlessly pursue what many would deem impossible. Remember, you possess more potential and capacity than you can currently fathom. As Steve Jobs insightfully remarked, we often overestimate what we can do in a year but grossly underestimate what we can achieve in ten years. Now, imagine doubling or tripling that span. The 20-year mark becomes not just a time frame but a canvas for monumental achievement.

Now take it a step further. Be specific. What specifically do you want to see in your life? Here's how to frame this vision:

- **To Have**: What possessions signify success to you? Is it owning a portfolio of properties across the globe, or perhaps having the financial freedom to pursue your passions without constraint?

- **To Do**: Consider the actions you want to take or the experiences you wish to have. Do you see yourself traveling the world, starting philanthropic ventures, or maybe mentoring the next generation of investors?

- **To Be**: Who do you want to become? This could relate to your personal development, professional status, or the impact you want to have on your community.

- **To Give**: What contributions do you want to make to the world? Think about the legacy you aim to leave behind, not just in terms of wealth but in the value you've added to society.

- **What about Family**: Envision the future you want for your family. What foundations do you want to lay down for them? How do you see your success enriching their lives? What is your role? How are their lives impacted by yours?

STEP TWO: ASSESS YOUR CURRENT POSITION

Understanding where you are right now is as crucial as knowing where you want to go. This step is about taking an honest look at your current state in the real estate investment journey. It's about assessing your resources, your knowledge, and your experience. Identifying your starting point allows you to tailor the journey ahead, ensuring each step you take is aligned with your ultimate goals.

WHERE ARE YOU NOW?

- **No Capital**: Starting without capital is a common challenge but not an insurmountable one. Your focus should be on strategies for capital raising in the first 2 years. This might involve saving from your current income, exploring partnerships, or learning about creative financing options like wholesaling or lease options that require minimal initial investment.

- **Some Capital and Experience**: If you're here, you've likely made a start but are looking to grow. The next phase should focus on Building Wealth through Rental Portfolios. This 4-year period is about leveraging your existing capital into rental properties that provide steady cash flow and appreciation. Focus on learning about property management, tenant acquisition, and scaling your portfolio.

- **Accredited Investor**: As an accredited investor, you have a unique set of opportunities and challenges. Your path can include more advanced investment strategies from the outset. Consider dedicating the next phase of your journey to multifamily investments or commercial real estate, areas that can offer significant returns but require a deeper understanding of the market and larger capital outlays.

INTEGRATING BOOK CONCEPTS

Irrespective of your starting point, the concepts and strategies outlined in this book serve as a guide to elevate your real estate investment journey. Following the structured approach detailed in the chapters ahead provides a roadmap that is both proven and adaptable to your unique circumstances.

MAKING IT ACTIONABLE

- **No Capital**: Start with enhancing your financial literacy and understanding the real estate market. Network with potential investors and learn about different types of real estate investments. Your immediate goal is to find a way to get into your first investment. If you've never done a Flip before, you can easily do 3-4 over the next year. Then the next year plan to triple that number. You can do that without even quitting your day job.

- **Some Capital and Experience**: Focus on identifying potential rental properties that align with your long-term goals. Work on refining your investment criteria, conducting thorough market analysis, and building a team to support your expanding portfolio. Chose a strategy defined in the Chapter 3.

- **Accredited Investor**: Explore opportunities in multifamily or commercial real estate that may not be available to the general public. Consider partnerships, syndications, or direct investments that leverage your capital and experience for higher returns.

STEP THREE: BREAK IT DOWN - MAPPING OUT THE PATH

Embarking on a 20-year quest to build your real estate empire and secure a lasting legacy requires not just vision, but a meticulously crafted plan to make that vision a reality. To transform your lofty dreams into tangible achievements, let's dissect this journey into manageable milestones and objectives.

10 Years Out

Halfway through your journey, the 10-year milestone serves as a critical checkpoint. It's here that the compound effect truly begins to manifest, demonstrating that your consistent efforts are starting to accelerate your progress exponentially. By this point, you shouldn't expect to be halfway to your 20-year goal; rather, thanks to the nature of compounding, being about 1/5th of the way there is a more realistic and still impressive achievement. This milestone is a testament to the power of persistence and the exponential growth that comes from compounded actions. It's a time to reflect on the progress made and to recalibrate for the journey ahead, ensuring that every step continues to build upon the last.

7 Years Out

Just before reaching the halfway mark, your 7-year goals act as pivotal moments of growth and expansion. These goals are designed to significantly advance your journey, setting the stage for the compounding effects that will become more pronounced in the years to follow. This might involve expanding your portfolio, delving into new types of real estate investments, or solidifying your position in the market.

3 Years of Annual Goals

To navigate from where you are now to your 7-year goals, break down your plan into annual objectives for the next three years. These yearly goals should be specific, measurable, and achievable, each one building on the last and steering you towards your longer-term ambitions. This granular approach ensures that your actions are aligned with your overarching strategy, allowing for incremental progress that feeds into the larger vision.

Quarterly Focus

Divide each year into quarters, focusing on a singular goal for every 12-week period. This timeframe is optimal for the human brain, balancing the fine line between achievable and challenging. It's short enough to maintain focus and long enough to achieve something meaningful. Setting and achieving these quarterly goals fuels your momentum and confidence.

Daily Actions

The true transformation happens in the daily grind. Every day, identify a single, critical activity that aligns with your quarterly goal. Writing down this daily task, along with your 12-week objective and annual goal, reinforces your commitment and focus. The act of writing—not just reviewing—this trio daily ingrains your path in your mind, keeping you relentlessly aligned with your larger vision.

Consistency and Adaptation

Regularly review your progress every 12 weeks, adjusting as necessary but always keeping your ultimate dream in sight. This isn't just about hard work; it's about smart, strategic, and sustained effort. Your roadmap isn't rigid; it's a living plan that grows and adapts with you.

The Essence of Change

Remember, the essence of change lies not in sporadic leaps of effort but in the small, daily actions that accumulate over time. It's these actions, consistently performed, that compound into the extraordinary life you've envisioned. Your 20-year roadmap is more than a plan; it's a commitment to a lifestyle of continuous growth and achievement. Dream big, start small, but most importantly, start now.

TAKE ACTION NOW

What sets the successful apart from the unsuccessful can be distilled into three simple, yet powerful words: ***take action now.*** This mantra is more than just a call to progress; it's a directive for transformative change, a catalyst for realizing the dreams you've dared to dream. As you stand at the threshold of embarking on a 20-year journey that promises not just growth but a legacy, the distinction between dreaming and achieving rests on your willingness to act.

The path laid out in this book is your blueprint. Yet, a blueprint alone does not build a legacy; action does. It's time to move from the conceptual to the tangible, from planning to executing. And you don't have to do it alone. The Long Game Community awaits you—a collective of dreamers turned doers, all guided by the shared vision of making their 20-year plan a living reality.

Joining The Long Game Community is your next step, a decisive action that bridges the gap between where you are and where you want to be. Inside, you'll find not just personalized assistance, coaching materials, and instructional videos to navigate your journey, but also camaraderie, support, and the shared wisdom of those who walk the path with you.

So, as you turn this new page in life, remember that the journey ahead is not just about the goals you've set but about the steps you take to achieve them. Take action now. Join The Long Game

Community. Engage with the resources, connect with your fellow travelers, and start transforming your 20-year vision into reality.

Your future self will thank you for the actions you take today. Let's embark on this journey together, making each step count toward building a legacy that lasts.

SCAN HERE TO JOIN THE LONG GAME COMMUNITY AND KICK-START YOUR JOURNEY TO TRUE LASTING WEALTH

GLOSSARY OF TERMS

- **1031 Exchange**: A tax strategy allowing an investor to defer capital gains taxes by reinvesting the proceeds from the sale of an investment property into another property.
- **Adjusted Gross Income (AGI)**: Your gross income after adjustments have been made. It determines your eligibility for certain tax deductions and credits.
- **Adjustable-Rate Mortgage (ARM)**: A mortgage with an interest rate that can change over time, based on a market index.
- **Amortization**: The process of spreading out a loan into a series of fixed payments over time, covering both principal and interest.
- **Appreciation**: The increase in the value of a property over time due to various factors, including market conditions, renovations, and changes in the surrounding area.
- **Assessment**: The valuation of property for the purpose of taxation.
- **BRRRR**: An investment strategy that stands for Buy, Rehab, Rent, Refinance, Repeat. It involves purchasing a property,

improving it to add value, renting it out, refinancing it to recover the renovation costs, and repeating the process.

- **Bridge Loan**: Short-term financing used until a person or company secures permanent financing or removes an existing obligation.

- **Capital Expenditure (CapEx)**: Funds used by a company to acquire, upgrade, and maintain physical assets such as property or equipment.

- **Capital Gains**: The profit from the sale of a property or an investment, potentially subject to capital gains tax.

- **Capital Gains Tax**: A tax on the profit realized on the sale of a non-inventory asset that was greater than the amount realized on the sale.

- **Cap Rate (Capitalization Rate)**: A measure used to assess the profitability and potential return on investment of a real estate investment, calculated by dividing the property's annual net operating income by its current market value.

- **Cash Flow**: The net amount of cash being transferred into and out of a property, especially as it relates to income-generating properties. Positive cash flow indicates that a property is generating more income than it is incurring in expenses.

-

Closing Costs: Fees and expenses, over and above the price of the property, incurred by the buyer and seller during the real estate transaction.

- **Commercial Real Estate**: Property used solely for business purposes, as opposed to residential real estate.

- **Conforming Loan**: A mortgage that meets the purchasing criteria of government-sponsored enterprises such as Fannie Mae and Freddie Mac.

- **Cost Segregation Study**: An analysis conducted to identify and reclassify personal property assets to accelerate depreciation deductions, thereby reducing taxes owed.

- **Debt Service Coverage Ratio (DSCR)**: A measurement of a property's cash flow available to pay current debt obligations.

- **Deed**: A legal document that represents the ownership of real estate.

- **Depreciation**: An accounting method used to allocate the cost of a tangible asset over its useful life. In real estate, it's used for tax purposes to deduct the costs associated with buying and improving a property.

- **Due Diligence**: The comprehensive appraisal of a business or property, by a prospective buyer, to establish its assets and liabilities and evaluate its commercial potential.

- **Due-on-Sale Clause**: A clause in a mortgage that requires the full payment of the loan if the property is sold before the mortgage is paid off.

- **Easement**: The right to use the real property of another for a specific purpose.

- **Effective Tax Rate**: The actual rate you pay on your taxes, as a percentage of your overall income.

- **Equity**: The difference between the current market value of a property and the amount owed on any mortgages or loans against it.

- **Equity Skimming**: An illegal scheme involving investors using inflated appraisals to extract cash from properties, typically leaving them in foreclosure.

- **Escrow**: An arrangement where a third party holds and regulates payment of the funds required for two parties involved in a given transaction.

- **Estate Tax**: A tax on the transfer of the estate of a deceased person. The estate tax is applied to estates for which the value exceeds an exclusion limit set by law.

- **Exemption**: A portion of income that is not subject to tax and can be used to reduce a taxpayer's taxable income.

Fair Market Value (FMV): An estimate of the market value of a property, based on what a knowledgeable, willing, and unpressured buyer would likely pay to a knowledgeable, willing, and unpressured seller in the market.

- **Fix & Flip**: A real estate investment strategy involving the purchase of properties at a low price, renovating them, and then selling them for a profit.
- **Foreclosure**: The action of taking possession of a mortgaged property when the mortgagor fails to keep up their mortgage payments.
- **Gentrification**: The process of renovating and improving a house or district so that it conforms to middle-class taste, which can lead to the displacement of lower-income families and small businesses.
- **Green Building**: A structure that is environmentally responsible and resource-efficient throughout its life-cycle: from planning to design, construction, operation, maintenance, renovation, and demolition.
- **Hard Money Loan**: A specific type of asset-based loan financing through which a borrower receives funds secured by real property.
- **Home Equity Line of Credit (HELOC)**: A line of credit available to homeowners using the home's equity as collateral.

- **House Hacking**: A strategy where the investor lives in one of the units of their investment property and rents out the others, using the income to pay for the mortgage and other expenses.

- **Installment Sale**: A method of sale that allows the seller to defer gains over the period the buyer makes the payments, spreading out tax liabilities over time.

- **Interest Deduction**: The ability to deduct interest paid on any loans secured by a primary or secondary residence, which can include mortgages and home equity loans.

- **Interest-Only Loan**: A loan where the borrower is required to pay only the interest on the principal balance for a set term.

- **Joint Venture (JV)**: A business arrangement in which two or more parties agree to pool their resources for the purpose of accomplishing a specific real estate project.

- **Landlord**: The owner of rental property who permits another to use it in exchange for rent.

- **Leverage**: The use of borrowed capital or mortgage financing to increase the potential return of an investment.

- **Lien**: A legal right or interest that a lender has in the property of another until a debt owed by that person is paid off.

- **Liquidity**: The ability to quickly convert an asset into cash without significantly affecting its price.

- **Loan-to-Value Ratio (LTV)**: A financial term used by lenders to express the ratio of a loan to the value of an asset purchased.

- **Marginal Tax Rate**: The rate at which your last dollar of income is taxed, representing the tax bracket into which your last dollar of taxable income falls.

- **Market Value**: The current value of a property determined by what a willing buyer would pay a willing seller in an open and competitive market.

- **NOI (Net Operating Income)**: A calculation used to analyze real estate investments, representing the total income a property generates after deducting all necessary operating expenses.

- **Non-recourse Loan**: A type of loan that is secured by collateral, usually property, but for which the borrower is not personally liable.

- **Operating Expenses (OPEX)**: The ongoing costs for running a property, excluding financing costs.

- **Opportunity Zones**: Designated geographic districts where investments are eligible for tax-advantaged treatment to spur economic development.

- **Passive Income**: Income resulting from business activities in which the person does not actively participate, such as rental income.

- **Portfolio Loan**: A loan that is held by a lender in its investment portfolio and not sold in the secondary market.

- **Pre-approval**: A lender's conditional agreement to lend a specific amount to a borrower based on certain criteria and a credit check.

- **Principal**: The original sum of money borrowed in a loan, or put into investment, separate from the interest.

- **Private Mortgage Insurance (PMI)**: Insurance that a lender may require from a borrower who has a down payment of less than 20 percent of the home's purchase price.

- **Property Management**: The operation, control, maintenance, and oversight of real estate and physical property. This can include residential, commercial, and land real estate.

- **Rate of Return**: The gain or loss on an investment over a specified period, expressed as a percentage of the investment's cost.

- **Real Estate Agent**: A licensed professional who arranges real estate transactions, putting buyers and sellers together and acting as their representative in negotiations.

- **Real Estate Broker**: A step above a real estate agent, a broker has more training and can work independently or have other agents work for them.

- **Real Estate Investment Trust (REIT)**: A company that owns, operates, or finances income-producing real estate, allowing investors to invest in portfolios of real estate assets.

- **Real Estate Professional Status (REPS)**: A tax classification allowing individuals who spend a significant amount of time in real property businesses to deduct all their rental loss against other types of income.

- **Refinancing**: The process of replacing an existing mortgage with a new one, typically with better terms or to take out cash against the equity built up in the property.

- **Rental Yield**: The annual rental income from a property divided by the property's current market value, usually expressed as a percentage.

- **Return on Investment (ROI)**: A performance measure used to evaluate the efficiency or profitability of an investment or compare the efficiency of several different investments.

- **Self-Directed IRA**: A type of IRA structure that allows the investor to make a broader range of investments, including real estate, beyond traditional stocks, bonds, and mutual funds.

Self-Employment Tax: A tax consisting of Social Security and Medicare taxes primarily for individuals who work for themselves.

- **Short Sale**: A sale of real estate in which the net proceeds from selling the property will fall short of the debts secured by liens against the property.

- **Standard Deduction**: A fixed dollar amount that reduces the income you're taxed on. Your standard deduction varies according to your filing status.

- **Tax Bracket**: Ranges of income to which different tax rates apply. The bracket determines how much tax will be applied to your taxable income.

- **Tax Credit**: A direct reduction of tax liability, not merely a reduction of taxable income.

- **Tax Deduction**: Expenses that can be deducted from adjusted gross income to reduce taxable income and thereby reduce the tax liability.

- **Tax Lien**: A legal claim by a government entity against a noncompliant taxpayer's assets.

- **Taxable Income**: The amount of income used to calculate how much tax an individual or a company owes to the government in a given tax year.

- **Title**: A legal document evidencing a person's right to or ownership of a property.

- **Title Insurance**: Insurance that protects the holder from financial loss sustained from defects in a title to a property.

- **Underwriting**: The process by which lenders evaluate the risks of lending money to a buyer and establish the terms of the loan.

- **Vacancy Rate**: The percentage of all available units in a rental property, such as a hotel or apartment complex, that are vacant or unoccupied at a particular time.

- **Valuation**: The process of determining the current worth of an asset or a company.

- **Variable Interest Rate**: An interest rate on a loan or security that fluctuates over time because it is based on an underlying benchmark interest rate or index.

- **Vendor Take-Back Mortgage**: A type of mortgage where the seller of the property provides financing to the buyer for the purchase of the property.

- **Wholesaling**: A real estate investment strategy involving the contract acquisition of a property with the intention of selling the contract to another buyer at a higher price before closing.

Withholding Tax: An amount that employers withhold from employees' salaries and pay directly to the government as a part of the employees' tax liabilities.

- **Zoning**: Government (usually local) regulations regarding the use of private property, specifying the area in which residential, industrial, recreational, or commercial activities may take place.

ABOUT THE AUTHOR

Burke Atkerson, Co-Founder and Managing Partner at Impact Investment Partners in Colorado Springs, brings extensive experience in global media and content production to his role as CEO of Flip-Lift, where he assists investors across the nation with Turn Key Fix & Flip services. With a strategic focus on Acquisitions and Investor Relations, Burke excels in diversifying investment portfolios, especially through multi-family properties, maximizing returns by capitalizing on market dynamics in a fluid real estate market.

Beyond real estate, Burke is an author and leads a non-profit aimed at improving mental health among men, addressing the rising issues of loneliness, addiction, and suicide. His commitment to mental wellness complements his professional achievements, demonstrating a holistic approach to success and societal impact.

At the heart of Burke's life is his family, including his supportive wife and six children, which serves as both inspiration and foundation for his endeavors. Driven by a desire to create generational wealth, Burke's vision surpasses mere financial gain, focusing on enriching relationships. His pursuit of real estate success is intertwined with a deep commitment to family and community well-being, underlining his dual mission of fostering professional growth and nurturing lasting connections.

JOIN THE LONG GAME COMMUNITY

Made in the USA
Monee, IL
05 June 2024

59428717R00121